Achieving Incredible Results for English Learners: A Blueprint for Educational Leaders

BRAD CAPENER

Dedication

This book is dedicated to my children, Nate, Anneliese and Marcus – three strong, gifted individuals who inspire me

Table of Contents

Introduction

The Challenge Before Us

By 2050 the Census Bureau projects "that the Hispanic school-age population will increase by 166% ... (to 28 million from 11 million in 2006)." (Fry & Gonzales 2008). As a result there is a rapidly growing population of students arriving at the secondary school doorstep, many of whom lack the academic language necessary to be successful in high school and college and compete with their native English speaker, middle class peers. The vast majority of these learners are born in the United States, hear Spanish spoken in the home, and speak conversational English very well. Some of these students have low literacy in their native language, and many who come from homes of poverty are exposed to far fewer words in general than their native English middle class peers.

Often these students become disengaged in their studies and many seek to remain 'invisible' in class to avoid making mistakes, or for other reasons. The student I am describing typically has a gap when it comes to understanding academic English. They don't have the vocabulary necessary to thrive in secondary school and beyond, and many fail to see themselves reflected in the learning or in the school culture.

While this is an oversimplification of a group of varied and complex students, English language learners face myriad issues in secondary schools, including but not limited to low self-esteem, isolation and non-acceptance, lack of support from teachers and counselors, poor grades, struggles at home that prevent strong attendance or good study habits, and their districts need to address these issues. They need to address these issues and address them quickly because, one, it's the law, and two, these children represent a growing demographic that represents the future of this country. If we want our children to be prepared for the jobs of the 21st century, and to hand down the values of American Democracy, we need to ensure all children are given every opportunity to succeed and to dream. Given the large percentage of the population they represent, it is imperative that districts set up systems and do everything they can instructionally to reverse the opportunity and achievement gaps.

Many of these difficulties can be overcome by applying extreme focus to the needs of this group, coupled with strong communication between grade levels and among all key stakeholders, and a solid commitment by stakeholders to ensure their success. As noted by Claude Goldenberg of Stanford University:

> Everyone who has an interest in the well-being of these students—parents, community members, leaders, teachers, specialists and coaches, school and district administrators, school board members, and state and federal officials—must be involved and contribute to a comprehensive framework to support ELs' achievement if we are to make progress in closing the achievement gap that concerns us all. (Goldenberg 2015, p. 1)

Additionally, the effort in this regard needs to be monitored and evaluated along the way to allow for adjustments and fidelity of implementation.

Having worked as a Title III Education Specialist for the state of Oregon, and as the K-12 ESOL Coordinator in Salem-Keizer Public Schools, Oregon School District 24J, one of the largest districts in Oregon (a state with exponential growth of ELs), I have seen districts around the state struggle with how to lift these students to a higher level of achievement. While I do not claim to have a magic bullet or the one solution to solve these challenges, I believe that solutions are possible and attainable, when done collaboratively and with fidelity and complete resolve.

While presenting at an English learner conference, my co-presenter and I discussed how to construct and organize professional development initiatives in a way that resonates with teachers of English Learners. After I gave the overview of our district's English Learner Education (ELE) vision document—our blueprint—as part of our presentation, multiple people approached me and said that this was exactly the kind of information they had been seeking at a conference and they were excited to bring it home to their districts. I realized that there are many hard working professionals working to improve the education of English learners but who feel overwhelmed by the many initiatives facing them. Many want to succeed but they, their districts, and their limited resources are pulled in many directions. Creating an ESOL Blueprint can ease the burden on teachers and schools by helping a district determine where to place focus and resources as well as how to implement the new initiatives in a measured, comprehensive way so that they prove successful.

This book is intended as a guide for district leaders, EL committee members, and other stakeholders with vested interest in EL success in creating a structure or framework, a blueprint, that has the potential to make significant headway in tackling the challenges associated with educating ELs. Just as builders need to assemble their raw materials to build a house, so too does district administration when planning and constructing a strong and effective English Learner Education Plan.

Each chapter in this book presents information and implementation ideas that work together in concert to inform your district's unique processes and needs: the book is not intended to be prescriptive. Rather, it is intended to provide you with a knowledge of ELs and their struggles, access to relevant research, and a description of the blueprint-creation process. The end goal for this book is to provide the guidance you and your district need to create a unique plan that is customized to your needs—to go through the process of designing a detailed blueprint for EL achievement.

Likewise, each chapter seeks to provide a foundation of knowledge for all educational leaders, regardless of their experience with ELs, in order to give everyone a solid and common understanding of the laws and issues pertaining to their education. Finally, each chapter also contains relevant interactive activities that can be used to spark discussions in your blueprint creation process.

When educators enter into this very intensive collaborative process focused on the success of ELs, great ideas will emerge, and the ensuing dialogue can promote action and sustainable planning that will truly solve many of the challenges facing our students trying to master academic English

The Backstory of This Book

I entered the field of English Learner education in Oregon during a time when it was becoming increasingly clear that more energy and focus was needed to make sure English Learners were being well served. As a state, Oregon has traditionally been a place lacking diversity and lacking a core understanding of what it means to come from another culture or possess a different language other than English. Over the past 15 years, however, the demographics have been changing significantly. While Oregon is generally viewed as a welcoming state and open to diversity, few school districts know how to best serve students who are acquiring a second language, and concepts like equity - the idea that ALL students will truly reach benchmarks and districts, schools, and teachers will make the necessary adjustments to ensure all students succeed both academically and socially-emotionally - are only now being explored at different levels by some districts.

It was during these beginning stages of awareness in Oregon - before equity was on the lips of superintendents and others - that I took the helm of largest English For Speakers of Other Languages (ESOL) Program in the state, in Salem. Having just come from the Oregon Department of Education where I was traveling around the state helping districts develop and improve their

ESOL programs and monitoring for compliance with state and federal laws, I now inherited a district that had spent very little attention on their secondary program. The elementary schools, by contrast, did have a coordinator and they were working very intently with Dr. Kathy Escamilla in implementing an Early Exit bilingual framework called Literacy Squared in about 22 schools. But the secondary schools had no district focus, which is why they brought me on board.

To understand the origins of this book, I think it's important to discuss the conditions under which English Learners in Salem-Keizer's existed in 2010, how I came to create the idea of an ESOL blueprint, and how I used it to give our program structure and vision. Hopefully the ideas in this book will resonate with districts around the country because as most everyone seems to be experiencing a similar influx of English Learners and looking for ways to best serve these students.

The first hurdle I encountered involved structures. Having not had a full-time coordinator for secondary schools, one can imagine that processes were either not in place or drastically outdated. I spent the first year updating procedures and policies, ensuring that our processes were compliant with Title III law and state law. I wrote explicit job duties for key staff who supported English Learners. I spent the first year going to schools and establishing relationships – listening to the challenges and using their input to put procedures in place. I also spoke at staff meetings – showing our district EL data and their school data to show that the need to support and focus on ELs was real and imminent.

Related to schools, we had a series of 'sheltered' core classes in our high schools that replaced the regular core classes, so that ELs could have more language support and the teacher could go at a slower pace. My concern as I observed these classes, however, was that the standards they used were not the same as the non-sheltered classrooms, and that the rigor and expectations of the students were diminished as well. This proved to be the case as I interviewed teachers. Many told me that ELs would not make it outside of a sheltered classroom. They felt an obligation - a passion even - to protect and keep them in classes that they believed, were designed to help. This thinking was pervasive across the schools - with teachers not wanting ELs because they didn't think they could handle the rigor (or perhaps some of them didn't want to change the way they were teaching). Not subscribing to a deficit thinking approach, I disagreed and believed that our ELs needed to be engaged and challenged, so I quickly began the process of dismantling these classes. My mantra was: motivate and challenge ELs but make sure you support them in the process. You've got to do both.

Along with the sheltered classrooms, we had a long list of English Language Development (ELD) courses in our high schools because ELs needed to have a different course number when they didn't pass the state language assessment. Large numbers of our ELs were not passing the state language assessment and in order to give them more elective credits, the district had designed over six different ELD class offerings. Unfortunately, when I visited the higher level classes, I could not see a significant difference between them in terms of the curriculum - which was often the same or very similar to the other previous course. When I went into classes, students of different proficiency levels were placed together based on teacher recommendation. The instruction was often not engaging and failed to focus on building the academic language necessary for being successful in school. In short, ELs were being coddled and not challenged in the high schools. They built a system that kept them in ELD and a series of sheltered classrooms, and made it difficult for them to acquire the needed credits to graduate. In fact, in one high school they had a series of 'houses' one of which, was dedicated solely to ELs. This meant that they spent most of their day in the same hallway with the same peers, taking the same 'sheltered' classes.

The message they were unintentionally sending was that these students weren't as smart or capable as their non-EL peers. I spoke with many students and heard first-hand how they felt about themselves. One student remarked to me when I asked a group if they know why they are in an ELD class and if they know how to exit, "We're here because we're stupid." It broke my heart.

The professional development we were offering for content teachers, called SIOP, which stands for Sheltered Instruction Observation Protocol, was okay, but it didn't have the intended effects I would have hoped to see. In other words, after taking the three-day training, teachers weren't using the strategies or changing practice in how they planned or taught as a result of their new learning. I felt that some of our workshops were lacking engagement and relevancy and didn't really see the point of continuing something that teachers weren't using or finding helpful. As a result, we completely overhauled the way we offered professional development. For instance, instead of a three-day training, we spread the trainings out over a semester and placed a specialized coach at the school. Teachers would come to a training, receive engaging strategies and then go practice them in-between sessions. When they showed up to the next session, they would bring their evidence and their questions. If they needed support between sessions, they would reach out to the coach to model a lesson or gather more ideas. This process would last a semester, and then the second semester, we offered 'touchback' trainings in the building. The imbedded coach would lead the same group and work on going deeper with their knowledge and practice. For the teachers who took these trainings, we saw significant development in their skills and effectiveness. We also heard directly from them in person and in reading their evaluations, that they really valued the support and the quality of the trainings, which they said, were practical, helpful, and engaging.

It was the philosophy of the district at that time that the standards are the curriculum. In other words, few textbooks existed, each content area had a set of standards, and people had to create their own units to match the standards. For our ELD teachers, they had sets of old ELD textbooks, but everyone hated them (including the students) and no one used them. Teachers across the secondary schools were creating their own units in isolation of each other and it was common practice to have teachers develop units but not want to share them. My staff of specialized instructional coaches, called English Language Acquisition Specialists, were doing incredible work creating some units for teachers, but it wasn't enough. The need was much greater. New and veteran ELD teachers alike had no support and no way to improve. Given this environment, all ELD teachers were, for the most part, on their own and their knowledge base for how to teach ELD was troubling to say the least. Not only did they not have quality materials to draw from, they also had a lack of understanding about language acquisition and how an ELD class needs to be structured differently from a language arts class. In those days, most of our ELD teachers were also language arts teachers, and often treated the ELD class as an extension of their language arts class - giving more grammar, vocabulary worksheets, or novels with no structured language objectives or supports. We changed this by creating a series of district professional learning communities, wherein all district ELD teachers came together to learn best practice and plan quality units with their peers. I fought for and received permission to acquire new textbooks. We created an online support page where teachers would post their units and resources for all to share. We piloted books until teachers agreed upon the most engaging and relevant materials, and we purchased them. I then had my staff bring teachers together to plan units from these new textbooks and continue to learn about what quality ELD should consist of on a daily basis in classrooms. We created observation walkthrough tools and began having our coaches working with teachers using this form to help develop their practice. Our goal was simple: to become a strong, consistent team; to support our teachers to be their very best.

When it came to the social-emotional needs of our ELs, we had nothing in place to address them in 2010. All students were expected to conform to a traditional American school culture and instead of seeing potential, many teachers failed to challenge and support their students, or change their practice to help them succeed. It became readily apparent that many of our ELs felt like second-class citizens and received a very mediocre education. Few if any ELs were in advanced IB, AP classes. We had classes designed to help students prepare for college called AVID, but few if any ELs were in them. I had my team create Graduation Checklists and required all ELD teachers to incorporate the use of them into a unit in ELD class. This way, students could see what they had and what they needed to graduate on an ongoing basis. I created a long-term EL committee and worked with assistant principals and instructional coaches on understanding the issues and coming up with a plan to serve the student holistically. I called it, Continuity of Care.

I can continue to describe my program as I inherited it, but I think the point has been made. The conditions under which our ELs were being served back in 2010 were poor. We had no focus, many people operated under a deficit model of thinking in relation to ELs, and no systematic efforts had been made to resolve the issues until I was hired.

As a result of my efforts to make drastic change, I created what I called the ESOL Blueprint for Success. In this blueprint, I had major categories under which all of our improvement efforts were conducted. Today, we have made significant strides to improve the conditions for our English Learners. I cannot take the credit for all of the improvements, but I can say that our blueprint made an organized, systematic difference that has really helped change a culture in my district, and hopefully a difference in the lives our our cherished students.

This book is for you. The hope is that this process does for you what it did for me.

A Note on Acronyms Used in This Book

As you may be aware, we in education speak our own acronym-laden language. That didn't really occur to me until one evening when I went to a staff party at a teacher's house. The party included the spouses of the teachers, all of whom were in different professions—that did not use educational acronyms. I fondly remember one teacher translating for me as I sputtered a number of acronyms out in one sentence: "RTI is great for supporting the LRC and the EGC, but it's also applicable to ESL – especially L-TELS." The Oregon Department of Education was no better—we carelessly threw acronyms around in meetings as if it were some cruel game to see if people could follow the conversation. I was often lost and kept a 'cheat sheet' on my desk to help me.

English Learners work, with its own host of acronyms, is no less confusing. While acronyms are plentiful and change rapidly, I will be using them in the following manner:

ELE: English Learner Education

ESOL: English for Speakers of Other Languages. The overall program to help students who are learning to speak English.

EL: English learners. Students who are in the process of adding English to their linguistic repertoire.

ELD: English Language Development. The class students take to improve their language acquisition. While these classes are sometimes referred to as *ESL*, this book uses the term *ELD*.

LEP: Limited English Proficient. Term frequently used by the U.S. Education Department to describe English learners. It is only used in this book when government documents are quoted.

L-TEL: Long-term English Learner. English learner who has been in the ESOL program for multiple years.

How to Use This Book

In writing this book, I have two interrelated objectives: to inform district leaders about what it means to successfully serve ELs; and, assisting district leaders in creating a plan and guiding document to ensure ELs are ultimately successful in school and in life.

At the end of each chapter, I have one or two suggested activities for leadership groups. These activities are aligned to the objectives of the chapter and are meant to spark discussion and help structure a Program Review and a creation of an ELE Blueprint document with a 3-5 year plan. Please note that these activities are merely suggestions. Readers of this book may choose to create their own processes or focus on the content only. While an ESOL/ESL department or leader can benefit greatly from reading this book, it is really intended for an entire district leadership team. I have found that engaging in real, meaningful change for ELs, requires an 'all-hands-on-deck' approach.

Also note that this book can also be read out-of-order. It can be used as a book study and groups can focus on various chapters they find meaningful and pertinent to their situation. For example, evaluating one's ELD program can involve months of observations, discussions and evaluations. Perhaps district leadership would like principals to read this as a book study and focus on the *Leadership and Professional Development, ELD, and Content* chapters. Regardless, of how one wants to approach this work, the book is designed with the intent to be useful, practical, and readily accessible.

CHAPTER 1

Identifying Core Values

Chapter Objective:

To develop a set of core values that will guide the creation of an ELE Blueprint.

If you have purchased or received this book, you want to learn more how to improve English Learner Education (ELE), in particular systems, instruction, supports, and so on. You are also likely looking to build a district vision that everyone can understand, contribute to, and champion. When designing a plan to improve conditions for disadvantaged students, I believe it is imperative to begin by examining our core values with respect to education and student learning. Operating in this way puts students at the forefront of our thinking and planning at every turn. Readers of this book will undoubtedly have their own set of values when designing a plan, but I have included my own as an example and to help guide district planning and thinking.

Core Value 1: Equity

Moral imperative

Being an advocate for English Learners for the past 11 years, my experience has been that most educators I talk with have a great deal of heart and compassion when discussing their success. I frequently hear the words "equity" or "cultural responsiveness" used in sentences pertaining to professional development or described as a greater need for future work. I think so many school districts around the United States have been experiencing an influx of children whose primary language is other than English, that many of them are seeing the need for a more focused approach in addressing their needs. While the idea that more focus is catching on, it is... *not*... enough.

We as a community of educators have a moral imperative to make sure all English Learners have our continued and focused attention. These children are currently in our schools - many of them struggling both emotionally and academically. In a few short years, they will be graduating from our schools and going to work. How are we preparing them for the workforce of the future - one that looks very different from the outdated Industrial Revolution model of the 19th and 20th century? How are we promoting creativity, innovation and collaboration and setting them up for jobs that don't yet exist? How are we preparing them to be our doctors and engineers, and professors? Are we igniting their passion for learning? Moreover, to what extent are we passing the torch of American values, customs, and history to a significant percentage of young Americans who may currently feel unwelcome and unsupported? Surely, as Americans, we should all be concerned about our country's health as a thriving Democracy and a continued economic power.

Ensuring our English Learners are aiming for and thriving in higher education is not something we can ignore or incrementally address. We need to act as if next year is too late. From an economic standpoint, from a citizenship standpoint, it makes good sense. However, it goes beyond that. From a human standpoint, it becomes our moral duty.

Asset-oriented approach

Having an asset-oriented approach is a non-negotiable as you plan and implement your blueprint for EL success. An asset-oriented approach is seeing all students (not just ELs) as learners who bring something to the table, who have something valuable to share, build on, and contribute. For example, a child who came from Mexico in 4th grade and is now in a 7th grade world history class is trying to master both conversational and academic English as well as new content in this class as well as five or six others. Although he *may* be struggling when compared to his English only peers, he is still bright and wanting to be engaged and challenged. He also wants to contribute his knowledge and experience from his past and add to class discussions. Failure to recognize and plan for this is a potential missed opportunity to ignite a flame and passion for learning.

A large part to running an effective school involves every adult in the school believing that English Learners in a regular classroom setting have the ability to succeed at high levels with proper support. All teachers across the district's schools should genuinely believe that English learners are just as capable as their native-English speakers. This belief will be reflected in how they treat their students. Leaders should be modeling good cultural awareness and make equity a priority in everything they do and say, which will lead students to feeling more at home in the classroom. When teachers pull together to support ELs while challenging them with rigor and relevance, ELs feel that support, which will enable them to rise to that challenge. If the majority of your staff has a supportive growth mindset and approaches planning and instruction in a way that engages all ELs so they can be successful in accessing the content and language standards, ELs can feel successful and meet those standards.

I have in fact, interviewed many students over the past few years who have willingly expressed how happy they are with their ELD teacher. When I ask why, they often comment on the fact that their teacher takes an interest in them and values their experiences, their culture and their language.

In addition to seeing all students as bringing something to the table, the same goes for teachers. While there may be room for improvement in many of your instructors, each one has something important to offer. Work with what they have to offer, rather than being critical, and you will earn both their trust and respect.

Cultural Competency

Because ELs need supports and interventions that are closely tied to their cultural backgrounds, I'd like to address cultural competency and equity before talking about ways to help these students. *Cultural competency* refers to one's understanding of the background, values, norms, and characteristics of one's own culture and the culture of others. *Equity* refers to justice, fairness, and freedom from bias or favoritism. In EL education, we strive to be culturally competent because it leads to equity in education.

The Importance of Cultural Competency

With so many ELs struggling to graduate on time, I think we need to ask ourselves if we are doing enough to meet our students where they are in order to help them learn. Here is where cultural competence becomes a crucial element in an ESOL blueprint. Studies have shown that students respond better when teachers have an understanding and make use of the linguistic and cultural experiences and backgrounds of their students. (Wright, W. (2010)

In a video interview, education professor Geneva Gay from University of Washington–Seattle uses the image of a filter to explain that children are not blank slates when they arrive in our classrooms; their background, cultural heritage, ways of thinking, and experiences are completely different from those of other students. Essentially, they see the world through a filter. School systems also have a filter as well. They provide information to students through a filter of not only language, but culture as well. Culturally responsive teaching entails schools adapting and modifying the information they provide, rather than expecting students to adapt to the learning environment, so that students can more readily receive information through their unique cultural lenses.

Incorporating Cultural Competency

Now that we've established the need for cultural competence, the question then becomes one of what to do? What does adding cultural competency into your blueprint look like? It may seem burdensome to ask instructors to take on yet another thing, we can't afford *not* to include culture and respect for our children on a daily basis. Likewise, our teachers have full plates with multiple preps, lesson planning, grading papers, and learning new strategies to better themselves; but, we can't afford not to include culture into the mix – not if we are serious about having *all* students prepared for college and career.

Some districts go 'all in' and adopt a program for their entire staff, like the *Courageous Conversations about Race video program by Glenn Singleton. This is a video series based on Singleton's book, Courageous Conversations that allows teachers to watch and learn at their own pace.* Some bring in guest speakers or contract with outside agencies to provide a series of workshops. All of these ideas are great, but they can also take a lot of money and a considerable investment of time and focus; in truth, not everyone is in the position to do this for one reason or another.

So how can your district reach a higher level of cultural competency without a large outlay of cash or time? Let's examine these ideas of cultural competence and equity in light of educational systems. Note the context in which Cross, T., Dennis, K., & Isaacs, M. (1989), in their foundational work, define cultural competence:

> … cultural competence, is defined as a set of congruent behaviors, attitudes, and policies that come together in a system, agency, or among professionals and enables that system, agency, or those professionals to work effectively in cross-cultural situations. Operationally defined, cultural competence is the integration and transformation of knowledge about individuals and groups of people into specific standards, policies, practices, and attitudes…

This quote highlights some meaningful words that relate to systems thinking. "attitudes, and policies that come together in a system," and, "…integration…into specific…policies, practices." When I read these words, I think about the importance of changing the culture of a school. It's not enough to have celebrations of other cultures or pictures of Cesar Chavez and Martin Luther King on a classroom wall (although those are all good to have). It's more than that. From a leadership perspective it's about ensuring policies and practices, like suspensions and expulsions are fair, and if not, looking deeply into the reasons for this inequality and how to address the root causes. It's about bringing cultural competence to the forefront of professional learning throughout the year, perhaps at staff meetings, or in professional learning communities, data teams, and so on.

For the teachers, it's about everyone in the school sharing a common belief and attitude that every child can learn at high levels and ensuring everything can be done to ensure every child is reaching grade level benchmarks. It's about intentional unit and lesson planning that begins with the end goal in mind and works backwards from there to ensure all of the proper scaffolds are in place, like pictures, key vocabulary, and differentiated sentence frames as a few examples.

Attitude + UBD Planning

In relating equity to education, Linton and Davis (Equity 101, 2013, p. 18) write, "Equity is not about equal treatment of students, but equal – and equitable – educational results….equity occurs when educators provide all students with the individual support they need to reach and exceed a common standard."

In other words, when a school builds a culture of equity that says that all students will be prepared for graduation and given the skills to enter college and takes *all students* to mean just that – all students – then some reflection and focused dialogue may need to take part from the school staff.

Linton and Davis (2013) cite characteristics that teachers share in schools considered to be 'culturally proficient' include

- holding high expectations of all students;
- holding every child accountable for learning;
- making lessons engaging, interesting and fun;
- having a plan for those who are struggling;
- being understanding of the challenges students may face at home;
- connecting lessons to the cultures of their students.

These ideas provide an easy and inexpensive way for teachers to incorporate culturally proficient and responsive instruction into their classrooms. The teachers provide a clear focus on students and provide culturally competent instruction to ensure that all students achieve at high levels and reach mastery. By ensuring all students are learning, challenged, and supported to meet and exceed standards, your district will be on a significant path toward instructional equity.

Since we are about putting concrete steps into a Blueprint, I want to offer a few actionable ideas one could do to begin this process. Please understand that this is not a comprehensive list of ideas. As with anything in this book, ideas spark dialogue.

Salem-Keizer's Steps to Achieve Cultural Competency

The following are steps that Salem Keizer has taken to achieve cultural competency. These activities build knowledge about, awareness of, and sensitivity to other cultural realities.

District Conference: Create and facilitate a conference that focused on cultural identity, storytelling, and leadership. Provide students with powerful reaffirming messages and learned that "Your Voice Counts!" Salem-Keizer's event took place at a local university so middle and high school students could visit a university and see themselves attending.

Culture Guides: Develop and distribute literature about individual groups and cultures that are present in SK schools; administrators and teachers read and discuss these Culture Guides to build awareness about their students and families.

Book Study: Create a series of Book Groups at schools. Purchase books for teachers to read about being more culturally aware.

Administrator Training: Offer administrator trainings in the summer or beginning of the school year each year to refresh or enhance knowledge.

Administrator Walkthroughs: Organize a series of administrator walkthroughs using an observation tool to discuss desired outcomes in instruction.

Professional Development: Send teachers to The National Association of State Directors of Migrant Education (NASDME) annual conference (and other conferences) to become more aware about the needs of their students - as funds will allow and per district permission.

Core Value 2: Focused, Intentional and Results Oriented

If there is one message to get across in this book, it is this: The more focused and intentional you are as a system in supporting the academic and social-emotional success of your ELs, the more likely they will exhibit growth.

It's wonderful when a school can see great results for all students, but to make broad and lasting change across the district, the entire leadership team must agree and acknowledge that students acquiring English as another language, students with disabilities, and other disadvantaged students are *the* top priority. District personnel must work together as one team, embrace the challenges and create systems and connections that will continue over time, regardless of who is leading.

Finally, while prioritizing ELs as a group is very important, it means very little unless the district is focused intently on results. Are our efforts at supporting ELs working? How do we know? If not, then what changes do we need to make to change our results?

It's been my experience throughout my travels in visiting different districts, that many leadership teams voice the importance of equity and the need to make ELs a priority, and yet, over time, their data fails to change significantly, if at all. It has also been my experience that these well-intentioned districts are not actually focused, intentional or results oriented. Being results oriented means that you are constantly looking at your student data and evaluating your programs and making adjustments until you *see* the outcomes you want. It's about ensuring everyone is focused on EL success as a unit, all of the time. Supporting ELs requires a journey rather than a destination mindset - a journey that requires careful planning and attention to detail. If the data isn't showing growth and improvement, and if that growth and improvement isn't significant, then something is still wrong and needs immediate attention.

To better illustrate what it means to be focused, intentional, and results oriented, I visited four high poverty schools (one elementary, one K-8, and two high schools) that have significantly closed the achievement and opportunity gaps. I think it's important to include these interviews because one should know that it's more than just my opinion at play here. Some schools around the country are making great gains with their EL students and in the four I interviewed, although they are all very different, I found common threads in each that illustrate this core value of being focused, intentional and results oriented.

While each interview was lengthy and informative, for purposes of supporting this Core Value, I have distilled each one to include the essence of what each leader articulated as being the keys and methods to their success.

Aloha-Huber Park Pre-K-8 School
Beaverton, OR

Aloha-Huber Park Pre-K-8 school is located in Beaverton, Oregon. The school is comprised of 1000 students, 600 of whom are English Learners. They are at 85% poverty, have 53 ethnicities and 30 languages represented. For nine consecutive years, they have exited all ELs before entering high school. If that isn't significant enough, in looking at one year's state data in Oregon's 2017 Report Card, their ELs made more academic growth than any other school in the state of Oregon. They have, in fact, reversed the achievement gap and are out performing all of their title schools and most of their non-title schools. In fact, they tied Beaverton's top performing school, which has few ELs and low poverty, in terms of academic growth.

This is truly an impressive school; a school where the principal has received Principal of the Year, and a school that received the state's Carmen West Award in 2015 for showing significant gains for English Learners.

I sat down with the entire administrative team one morning and asked them to describe their success. The principal, Scott Drue said, "Brad, we are extremely intentional." He proceeded to show me how their school's data has grown over time and how it compares with the district and with the state. He said that when he first became principal of the school 12 years earlier, they had almost 100% staff turnover by his second year. They were the lowest performing school in the district and they had all kinds of problems. He struggled for several years to implement his vision, but eventually after a lot of hard work, they began seeing great gains in test scores and district leadership gave him the latitude he needed to implement the kind of program he wanted.

Fortunately, both he and his assistant principal, Alfonso Giardiello, have been teaming together for the entirety of those 12 years. Their instructional coach, too, was a teacher in the early years and is now their instructional leader and an integral part of their leadership team. So, consistency in having strong leadership appeared to be a common thread in Aloha-Huber, as well as in two of the other schools I visited.

Focus

When I asked Scott to describe their journey and break down their success into specific areas, he began talking about having a clearly defined vision and mission and consistently adhering to it over time. They believe in being very upfront with who they are as a school team and how they approach both instruction and how they support and challenge students. As such, Scott provided me with some of their literature and pointed to their set of Guiding Principles. "We have a set of core values that guide us and everything we do centers around our Guiding Principles. Totally non-negotiable." It was evident as I walked the halls and visited classrooms that these principles were not merely on paper, but incorporated as part of their culture.

Aloha-Huber Guiding Principles

- All adult actions impact student learning.
- Collaboration drives instructional practice within established systems.
- Teachers are responsible for 100% student engagement.
- Instructional practices are aligned and coordinated to support all students
- We operate in a complex and flexible system based on student need and proven practices.
- All students will achieve regardless of race, disability, SES, and all other variables

Intentionality

Hiring Staff

The art of hiring at Aloha-Huber Park is extremely intentional and one of their top priorities; it's a key reason, they would tell you, for their success. The administrators place great emphasis on hiring teachers with the right mindset - teachers who share the Aloha-Huber values and passion for teaching.

When Scott began his tenure at Aloha-Huber, he had to hire 30 teachers in his first year and about another 30 in the second. Teacher turnover was extremely high and morale was low. Over the years, however, and since Scott has been carefully and artfully attracting quality teachers, the attrition rate is now at 4%, which consists of retirements, teachers relocating, etc.

The new school was built in 2006 and Scott was allowed to build his own team over time. He decided to change how he hired staff and worked hard to keep only the teachers who were committed to growing and changing. He said, "Those who were not open to change were advised to move on or evaluated out of the profession." He talked about how hard that was at first with the union, but he had district support and stayed the course, true to his purpose.

Scott said, "We don't hire a teacher based on an interview. We watch them model a lesson and they go through an extensive debrief session with us. They have to sit through a 90 minute PowerPoint presentation of the school's professional expectations. We talk about the non-negotiables and the six guiding principles, and we typically meet candidates 3 or 4 times. In the final stage of the hiring process, we basically say, this is what what we will negotiate with you and this is what we will not negotiate with you." Since the reputation of the school is so strong now, top teacher candidates seek out the few openings that arise. They understand that it will be hard work, but they also know that they will be working with a strong team and well supported by leadership.

Building Teacher Leaders

As we spoke, I wondered how intentional Scott was in building teacher leaders, and to what degree that would make a difference in the success of his school. He responded, "As far as teacher leadership goes, that is an enormous part of our success. The 14-team and department leaders at Aloha-Huber Park make up our Instructional Leadership Team, and serve as the backbone of our instructional model. No major implementation or system adjustment at AHP happens without input from this team.

"Since we share kids, teacher teaming is a critical factor in our students' success. Team leaders are selected by solely the administration. We look for two critical qualities: 1. Demonstrated, sustained success as an instructor and 2. Universally respected by the staff.

"New team and department leaders are rotated into the instructional leadership team every few years to ensure a broad representation of AHP teachers' voices. All team and department leaders must attend the annual Aloha-Huber Park Leadership Seminar put on each Summer by the administration. This ensures members' clarity around our operating agreements, our school's Six Guiding Principles, as well as professional development to build capacity in teacher leadership (i.e. consensus building, difference between spheres of influence, tiered decision making, etc.)."

English Language Development

In looking at other areas of intentionality, I asked them about ELD and what that looks like at the school. They shared that all students get ELD and that all teachers are Language teachers. This is a non-negotiable. Scott continued, "You are a literacy teacher first. You don't have 'your' caseload of kids. You work with all kids. You teach all kids. You will teach all levels. You will work as a team and strategize as a team."

Cynthia 'Cindy' Kieffer, a Two Way Immersion Coordinator and Instructional Coach added, "Our ELD doesn't just happen during the half hour of focused ELD time. It's much more than that. Our General Education team hears that they are language teachers first. They are not just teaching math or social studies. We have an ESL team member helping each subject team with how to support language or intensive groups, and that is huge. It's a mind shift."

At Aloha-huber, all kids are together in classrooms. Students with Special Needs, English learners, all learn together and teachers differentiate according to their abilities. Because all kids can benefit from intentional language support, everyone walks to ELD according to their proficiency level and needs. "Teachers differentiate and group students in a way that allows all to be in the class and more importantly, feel successful about themselves in that class setting." Scott and his team spoke about the importance of all kids feeling successful, and not wanting ELs to feel like they have to go to a special class. "All students get ELD at the same time. All kids at our school need language development because we are a high poverty school. But they are grouped by their proficiency level and they are walked to their level. Pullout? Absolute barrier to success. The kids' self esteem is already low, their skills are not what they should be, but here, all kids are getting the same thing. They don't feel singled out. Here they don't know they are in ELD. They don't know they are in Special Ed. Even the white kids will say, 'I'm going to ELD.'"

In talking about secondary teachers, Cindy added, "Mindset is harder to shift with secondary teachers because they come in with a content specific mindset." Then Scott added, "Our guiding principles are what we focus on and we are very open and transparent with who we are." He added that these guiding principles have been very successful in terms of helping to change that mindset.

Additionally, and very importantly, they make a concerted effort at incorporating the ELP standards into the team planning process. Cindy said, "Continuity is really important, not to teach in isolation. Once we knew where the

ELA and priority standards were, then it was easy to add in the ELP stan-dards. They are very similar, and by showing teachers visually, graphically, what the standards are and how they relate to each other, it's easy to see how they relate and how the ELP standards can be integrated and focused on. So all teachers are now planning whole entire units using the ELP standards. And kids hear it once and it is reinforced later on in other classes. We also work the the language domains during that time as well."

Instructional Focus

I asked Scott and his leadership team if they had an instructional focus for the year, and if so, what was it and how was it determined? Scott quickly pulled out and handed me a postcard that succinctly described their instruc-tional focus for the year and said, "This is what we do."

Mr. Giardiello added, "We focus on three things. We hire the right people. We stay really focused, and we protect our teachers. This is key for us. We tell our teachers this is the only thing we are going to do this year." And Scott added, "And it was the same last year."

Mr. Giardiello added, "As an administrator you have to protect your teachers." He gave me an example of a new district math adoption and said it would be foolish to drop something that has been showing super gains in order to do something new and unknown. "So we are not saying no to the implementation, but we say, you know what, we have results with what we are doing. Give us time and we will add it."

Scott then added, "Because of our Guiding Principles, the district can come with any program, and we are not scared about that anymore." They just want the ability to be the sense makers for their staff and implement it in a way that makes sense for everyone, and doesn't overwhelm them.

Mr. Giardiello went on to explain another way they help their teachers stay focused on their craft. "We want our teachers to be in front of the kids. We don't want them at meetings, and doing things that don't relate to the classroom. We take away as much work from the teachers so they don't have to worry about that. As the administrative team, we assemble all of the data for them. We do all the paperwork, make all the copies, find the books they need, so teachers can just come to the meeting and talk."

Cindy then spoke more about how teacher time is structured and how the Guiding Principles help staff stay focused on the fact that they are here for the students. "It's hard and consuming work, but we don't just send teachers off to plan together. Now, whenever we meet, we have a plan and a structure, and we say today, during this time, we are going to focus on these four things, and we are going to make sure it's done and done efficiently, and here's the reason why. Providing the why and limiting the focus, makes it not so overwhelming initially."

Results Oriented

After visiting a series of classrooms, I entered into a staff room with data posted around the walls. Scott directed my attention to a chart labeled Guaranteed and Viable Curriculum, which asks the question, "How can we design effective instruction to maximize learning?" The chart showed their whole focused approach to instruction. It started by outlining standards and learning targets, and then went to identifying their common unit assessment with an attached rubric. The staff create the assessment from these targets and this assessment is a non-negotiable. From there they go into the lessons divided into three categories: Benchmark, where most students fall; Strategic, for those needing a little more help and support; and, the Intensive group that needs more intensive interventions. They create learning targets, and write out outcomes they want to see.

Mr. Giardiello said that the most important part of the chart is the analysis of the data and their response to what they find. "Teachers have to answer basically four questions:

What happened with the kids that met the standard? What happened to the kids that didn't meet? Why do they think they got this result? What are they going to do as a team to address it? The thing is, this is a team response. The students in the intensive class might not make benchmark, but the whole team of teachers gives input to that teacher to help him or her with what to do or try next. The success of the students is the team's responsibility, not the individual teacher's."

Scott added, "We are very open with our data. So we post names and percentages. Everyone sees the data. It took a while to get to this point, but we did. The philosophy behind this is that there is nothing to hide. We need to all work together as a team, and if the data isn't looking good in one area, or in a particular classroom, then the team assists and supports that teacher. It's now part of their culture, but it took a while."

From this process they track the data on a monthly basis. Scott said, "It used to be that we had to look at state testing data and hope for the best. Now we track what gains are being made on a monthly basis. We record what worked in this unit, what didn't."

Cesar Chavez Elementary School
Pre-K-5 Bilingual
Salem, Oregon

Chavez Elementary received statewide recognition for closing the achievement gap and academic gains for English Learners in a bilingual setting in 2018. With approximately 580 students, about 75% are minorities, with 67% being English Learners - primarily Latino - although there is a small but vital population of Pacific Islanders and Russian/Ukrainian students as well.

Olga Cobb was already a successful veteran principal when she was asked to open this school in 2012. I sat down with her to learn about her formula for success, and as we talked, she outlined multiple categories on a post-it note and both passionately and methodically began to convey her experience. To better convey the essence of our conversation, I've divided our discussion by the categories she chose to include as being significant to her success.

Focus

In our conversation, Olga talked about the necessity of being very focused on outcomes and building a strong school culture - one that stresses the importance of achieving academic results and building a strong school community where everyone, including parents, feel welcomed, honored, challenged and supported.

Since language support across the school is so important for English Learners' success, I asked her to elaborate on the ways they are intentional in achieving their outcomes and what language support looks like at Chavez.

Olga said, "We honor language in many ways. We do what we need to do for compliance. We follow the ELP standards to the letter. We focus on the ELP standards in our data teams. We have our 30 minutes a day of ELD. But that's not all. Our ELs are our ELs all day long. So how do we offer them the ability to practice language, socially, in recess, in PE, in reading, writing, and science? We support language throughout the day. Focusing on language is always at the top of our minds. We have our Common Core standards that we focus on, but our language standards are our number one goal."

I was impressed by this because not every school focuses on ELP standards throughout the day in every class and making it such a priority. I then asked her to speak to the ways they are intentional in achieving results.

Intentional

Protecting Instructional Time

Olga spoke first about the necessity of protecting her teacher's time so that they are freed up to teach and focus on instruction.

She said, "We protect instruction over everything. Our number one job is to protect our teachers. They have the hardest job and we need to support them with behaviors and they have what they need. We also do a lot of celebrations in the school because they need breaks. When they are functioning well and happy with their jobs, then we see results with the kids."

While that is great, I know that in the United States, districts often introduce new initiatives and change focus frequently. Teachers often feel the stress and pressure of having to learn and master multiple new programs and initiatives, so while protecting instruction sounded great, I wanted to know how she protects their time. Olga responded, "What I always tell my staff and others is that we'll do it the Chavez way. We don't tell the district that we won't embrace the new initiative or program, but we ask them to give us some time and I'll get the results. But I need to do it our way. I'll go to my leadership team and talk about it. We have our three goals and then this is how the new piece fits. I'll say, 'We're going to start with step one and this little piece. Do you think this is doable?' We do it the Chavez way but we are not afraid of change and we say, bring it. We are not afraid of growing, but it needs to fit our style and it needs to not kill us."

Building Teacher Leaders

It became apparent while I was listening to her that supporting teachers was a high priority and a reason for their success. I asked Olga to elaborate on how she builds a team that supports her vision for the school. She said, "I believe in finding opportunities for teachers to show leadership. When you let other people lead and you (as the principal) follow in those moments, you show them that you trust them. When you trust them to lead in a specific way, they will come back and follow you later during a big change. I will turn to a staff member at a meeting and say, "Okay, you are the expert here; tell us where we need to go from here." Of course, I meet with them before and plan with them, but when you put a person in a place like that in front of everyone, there is something that happens. Always finding leadership in people is super important. This goes for everyone, including instructional assistants."

We spoke more about staffing and I asked her how she gets all of her teachers to come along with the vision and focus of the school. She first addressed the importance of hiring the right staff. She said she was fortunate at Chavez because she opened the school and was able to hire all of her staff, which was really key to moving quickly. But prior to opening Chavez, she worked at another school in the district where she cultivated a school culture and got the same results with a staff she inherited. It just took several years to cultivate that success.

Olga: As a principal, hiring is one of the most important jobs. Again, having a culture in the school where teachers feel loved and supported and cared for. Because when teachers feel that, kids feel that.

Some people will feel the need to leave, and you have to be okay with that too. I had a teacher that told me that she couldn't work with me. I thanked her for her honesty and said that I could help her with that. Our focus is not for every teacher, but this is who we are. We are upfront with what teaching looks like at Chavez because we want to recruit and retain teachers who are open to our approach.

Focusing on the Individual

The staff at Chavez believe in looking at each child and addressing the needs of every child. "There is no child who goes unnoticed. We have worked hard with the staff to understand that the behavior does not represent the whole student. We address the behavior, but the student deserves our love and respect. This can be hard, especially when it happens daily and the teacher has another 29 students to teach, so we have developed systems to protect instruction. We then come up with a plan so that the student feels loved and cared for, and respected, listened to and valued. When you do this, kids respond. They want to feel loved and valued and when you are this way with them, they respond in kind.

I asked her to elaborate on the systems she has in place. "We implement PBIS (Positive Behavioral Interventions & Supports) school wide. Most students fall within what we call, the green zone, where you might have to correct them once and they respond. Then you have the kids in what we call the yellow zone, who need a little more support and accountability. Finally, you have the students who fall in what we call the red zone, who need a lot more support." Olga shared that they started the year with 16 students in the red, which meant that they needed support throughout the day, sometimes all day, and currently she only has two remaining in the red zone. We have supports in the classrooms; positive calls home; meetings with parents. It's part of PBIS, but regardless of PBIS, it's about establishing a climate and culture that we value our kids and take them, and love them and accept them as they are."

Parent Outreach and Inclusion

Throughout our talk, Olga stressed the importance of cultivating a school identity that is purposeful and welcoming. She described how she wants parents to identify with the school. "To get the results we have, I can tell you with a 100% certainty that we would not be able to do it without the parents working with us. We try every year to bring parents in and buy into the goals of their children; participate in all aspects what we do. We honor their culture and we honor their background; we are richer because of the students that we have and because of the backgrounds that we have."

Since Chavez Elementary has a significant number or Marshallese, Chuukese and Russian/Ukrainian students as well as Latino students, she added, "In the beginning, we were learning about Marshallese and Chuukese students and their culture. That learning was important because we wanted to ensure those families felt welcome at the school. We started out with one Russian family coming to events. When we asked that family how we could get more families to come, they said, come to our church. You need to connect with the mom's and to the dads who drop off their kids. Because they need to know they can trust you." Olga listened and followed that advice. Now at her Bingo Nights, she has 6-700 families attend - and a thriving Russian community. But that wouldn't have occurred if she hadn't made the efforts.

Results Oriented

Olga and her team focus on results and use Data Teams as a means of tracking those results. Meeting in teams regularly to look at data, ask questions of themselves and discuss approaches and strategies is making a difference in how they approach instruction and provide supports. It was clear after talking with her, that over time the culture of the school has developed into one where teachers not only talk about good instruction and supports for students, but one where they need to see evidence that what they are trying is amounting to increased student achievement.

McMinnville High School
McMinnville, OR

McMinnville High School resides in the town of McMinnville, which is set in the heart of Oregon's Willamette Valley. Its total student enrollment is just under 7000, with about 34% of its student body self-reporting as Latino. According to the School Report Card, 95% of the student population is economically disadvantaged and about a third are ELs. In 2017, the Secretary of Education visited the school due to its high graduation rates and high standardized test scores, and wanted to learn about their excellent instructional practices. I too wanted to learn about their instructional practices as well as the secret behind their success.

I sat down with the Assistant Principal, Veronica Chase, one morning and asked her to describe their formula for success. Not surprisingly, I listened to a story of focus, intentionality, and being driven by results. I divided our conversation into these three categories.

Focus

Veronica explained that their superintendent was very adamant about being focused on several initiatives and staying true to that direction over time. "It was hard at first, but the result is that we have a common language across the district. If we talk about Cornell Notes, for example, our Kinder teachers know about this as do our 12th grade teachers. The pendulum (of change) hasn't swung. It's been steady for the past 12 years."

At one point during this time, a wellspring of teacher voices advocated for EL Achieve's Constructing Meaning (CM) to be a primary focus for the district, and the district listened and supported that as a primary direction. CM supports all learners, or course, but especially EL's in their content classrooms, by providing all teachers (regardless of subject area) with the strategies on how to scaffold instruction for those acquiring language. As such, roughly, 70% of the high school teachers use CM, and the training continues each year allowing them the opportunity to practice and go deeper with their knowledge and abilities to instruct in this manner. Veronica added, "People were seeing immediate results in what students could do, say and produce." When asked if the training continues throughout the year, she agreed and said that professional learning is best when it's done over time instead of in a one or two training scenario. "We have embedded staff development time regularly where we reinforce the concepts of CM. While some teachers attended the full CM training, others get pieces of that training during staff development time. Teachers are in different places in their implementation, but we provide and use this common language, and common strategies, which I think is really important."

In continuing our discussion on being focused, I asked her to explain how they got teachers to agree to changing their practice perhaps, by adding language supports and careful planning with ELs in mind. I knew that a core group of teachers requested that CM be a priority, but that doesn't mean all teachers want to change the way they approach instruction. Don't they have teachers who disagree with the direction or refuse to plan and add visuals, vocabulary, etc., to their teaching? How did they create a culture that focuses on ELs so intently?

Ms. Chase said, "The conversation first started by looking at our data. Here is how our ELs are performing. Are we okay with that? We had tough conversations about graduation rate data, test scores, how many ELs were accessing AP classes, and why our Latino students are underperforming. We have passionate teachers who want to help kids and when presented with the data, and asked these questions, they agreed that we needed to do more and came up with the solutions.

"To further support them, we provide common planning time and we fold in peer observations. It's hard for teachers not to change when they are observing a student of theirs who is not doing well, performing really well in a more scaffolded setting - It's hard to then say, I'm going to do it my own way."

I summarized our conversation and said, "So, administration presents that data and asks the touch questions. Then teachers work together to come up with solutions and the administration goes with that plan while ensuring that the vision and goals are being met and keeps the team focused throughout the year?"

Veronica responded, "Yes. There is no way the four of us (administrators) can come up with the solutions. We see through a certain lens, but it takes a village. Our teachers meet in data teams twice a month and each time we say, here's the data. Are we okay with this? What do we do about it?"

In addition to the professional development and common planning time, teachers receive,

Common Vision and Mission

McMinnville High School focuses on the following common vision and mission:

- Ignite Passion
- Pursue Purpose
- Rise to your worth

All conversations around improvement and the daily operations of the school revolve around these three focal points. When they discuss changes to curriculum or approaches to instruction, or supporting students, they always go back to their vision. Is whatever they propose during staff meetings or planning sessions focused around igniting passion in students, as well as teachers? Will it help students rise to their worth? Doing this repeatedly ingrains into the culture of the school to the point that it is a grounding focal point.

Guiding principles

Beyond the vision and mission, McMinnville uses the following guiding principles constantly in every meeting, discussion and decision:

What does the data say?

What do our students say?

Equity of opportunity - ensuring that barriers are removed to allow more students access to opportunities.

They value the student voice, ensuring, as Veronica says, that "students are 'at the table' and part of the conversation."

Intentionality

Data Teams

Ms. Chase spoke to being very intentional with Data Teams, which is essentially a process grade level or content specific teams engage in on a regular basis throughout the year. This process typically involves teachers deciding on a common unit or lesson, or skill they want to teach and connecting them to standards. They do a pre-assessment and track that data, decide on strategies, teach and come back as a group to look at their data to see how their students achieved. After looking at their post-assessment data, they make decisions about whether they have to re-teach the lesson in another way, or if they can move on. This focus on data was common in every school I interviewed.

Team planning

McMinnville High School is also intentional in providing teachers time to learn and plan, and in observing one another in a structured and safe environment. Ms. Chase spoke to an explicit focus for the last three years on all teachers becoming language teachers, or supporting and scaffolding language in their lesson planning and delivery; and, she spoke to being very focused on English Language Proficiency Standards in addition to the Common Core State Standards. When it comes to initiatives and protecting teachers so that they can focus and not feel overwhelmed, Veronica said that they create a grid on the whiteboard and post it at every staff development opportunity. This grid shows the initiatives they use, like CM. If they are introducing a new strategy that may not be CM specifically, the presenter purposefully goes over and marks the grid to show how it relates to their focus. Ms. Chase said, "We talk about effective practices regardless of what program that comes from. But many of the effective practices relate so we want to be very intentional and show how they are connected."

Staff Retention

Another example of intentionality at McMinnville High School relates to staffing - both in recruitment and in retention. The teacher retention rate is extremely high and Ms. Chase said, "We are very intentional about ensuring our teachers feel connected and satisfied in their jobs. We have a Career and Technical Education (CTE) daycare center on campus and our teachers are able to have their children in that program during conference time, for example. We also have a room set aside for nursing mothers. Those are just two little examples, we have many others, but really we care about the wellbeing of our teachers which we believe lends to student success."

It was evident too, as she described how teachers are supported in their own learning and growth, and how they are allowed to focus and develop their craft, that they would be happy and want to stay. Longevity and contentment of staff at McMinnville, Chavez, and Aloha-Huber seemed to be a common thread that each administrator felt contributed to their success.

Teachers also had common planning time and appeared to have a voice in the direction and development of their school, which was nice to hear since that is not always the case.

As we spoke about supporting teachers, Veronica added another lens they use to develop a staff culture - the lens of equity and mindset. The example she provided pertained to the label 'sheltered' classroom. Instead of having a 'sheltered' social studies class, for example, designed for ELs with low English skills, they refer to the class and to the student as accelerated. "We believe in a growth mindset, so we shifted that name because we believe the language we use sheds light on deeply held beliefs. It's now used without a thought. Sometimes you can shift words and practice to shift your mindset." Veronica felt that this simple shift in language had a positive impact on both staff in how they thought of their ELs, and on the students in how they viewed themselves.

Hiring and Placing Staff

From there our conversation went to hiring staff. I wondered if they were intentional about this as well because it seemed to be a common pattern in the schools I was interviewing. Veronica was emphatic about the importance of hiring the right people. She said that they were intentional about shifting their interview questions to seek candidates who, in their opinion, have the right mindset. "We are purposefully upfront with who we are and what we value when we hire.

We want to hire people who are passionate about teaching and have the right mindset; because it's easier to grow skill set than mindset. It always strikes me when a candidate says, I teach students instead of a particular subject."

In placing staff in assignments, we talked about the importance of putting strong teachers with ELs. "Our teachers are passionate about teaching ELs, but we bluntly state that we don't make teacher assignments based on seniority, but where they are needed." She added that they definitely have purposeful conversations with staff and have to be very proactive with their communication before they make schedule changes.

Continuity of Care

While the idea behind Continuity of Care, which essentially means taking care of the individual child and their needs, has a prominent place in this book, it's not always a piece that comes up naturally when talking about school improvement. The conversations often focus around instruction, curriculum, test scores and intervention classes. However, with each school I included in this section, the intentional efforts to support the individual child was very apparent and came up naturally without my asking. Ms. Chase said, "We spend a lot of energy focusing on each individual. We have trained classified staff regularly go over transcripts for each grade level and looking to see who is struggling. They identify students who are struggling, make calls home, and talk with the individual student. We also have one counselor who focuses on ELs specifically, and our Freshman Team is given the responsibility for supporting our ELs and their success. Any newcomer EL student that comes to us as a Sophomore, Junior, or Senior, meets with an administrator and we talk about their goals and make a plan for graduating."

School Culture

Finally, in talking about the ways they are intentional in supporting ELs, Ms. Chase talked about the importance of having a strong school culture dedicated to the success of all students, and making sure that ELs and students with disabilities are not an afterthought. "We schedule EL and Students with Special Needs first in master schedule. We want to make sure they have elective opportunities and placed in the right classes. We also have the pictures of each student who graduated posted along the walls, showing what college they are attending. Underclassmen are inspired by those they know, and think, 'I know that person. If they can go to college, I can too.'"

Results Oriented

The staff at McMinnville High School have a common vision, use common language and are intentional in how teachers are hired, how they receive support and are cared for, and given time to plan, learn and grow. They are intentional about placing students, using a growth mindset and ensuring each child is connected and looked after.

But is all of this working? How do they know and what do they do if it isn't? Many schools have mountains of data at their disposal, but what decisions are made based on that data? Being results oriented means that the school is focused on achieving goals and making the necessary adjustments along the way to ensure those goals are realized.

McMinnville High School has shown success in their growth. They are very intentional about all of their students, but they spend additional energy on ensuring their ELs are supported for success. They continually look at data and as a team, they ask hard questions and continue to challenge themselves. I don't think anyone at the school believes their goals are completed. In fact, Veronica shared that it's always to process that needs attention and refinement. But they are doing more than being focused around a few instructional strategies or having a common language. Schools can do those things and still have poor data. The key takeaway from this school is that they focus on adapting and changing to ensure their data improves. They are in fact, results oriented.

The table below identifies many of the shared practices that were discussed in the interviews as reasons for their success educating ELs.

FOCUSED	ALOHA HUBER	CESAR CHAVEZ	MHS
Clear & consistent vision and mission supported over time	X	X	X
Clearly defined and articulated goals	X	X	X
Guiding Principles	X		
Focused and protected instructional time	X	X	X
INTENTIONAL (How they reach the focus)			
Hiring practices	X	X	X
Teacher support retention, and celebrations	X	X	X
Building teacher leaders	X	X	X
Continuity of Care: supporting the needs of each child	X	X	X
Support with graduation plan	NA	NA	X
Parent inclusion		X	X
Honoring language and culture	X	X	X
Positive school climate and culture focused on supporting all students	X	X	X
RESULTS ORIENTED (How do we know our efforts are having an impact on learning and academic achievement)			

ELP Standards focused	X	X	X
Professional development that is ongoing, sustained and focused on growth	X	X	X
Data Culture where teams constantly evaluate relevant data results and make necessary adjustments	X	X	X
Common Planning Time with a focus on EL data and planning	X	X	X
OTHER			
Longevity of building administrators	X	X	
Longevity of district superintendent and being very focused on several initiatives over time that focus on EL success			X
District support in allowing school autonomy - trust in the administration	X	X	X
It is evident that Equity is a deeply held belief among staff; staff are passionate about ensuring ELs and all disadvantaged youth are high achieving	X	X	X
Strong, very structured and supportive leadership	X	X	X

Now that you have read how several administrators are making a difference for their English Learners, and studied at the table above to see where each school is similar in their approach, I want to comment briefly on several of the main ideas presented in this Core Value.

Clear and consistent vision

Each school I visited had a clearly articulated mission and vision that focused heavily on all learners, but made sure English Learners and Students with Special Needs are a priority in how they plan and teach. It was impressive to see that their vision was consistent over time and didn't vary from year to year. Also evident was a passion for equity and building in team planning time that required not only planning with ELP standards, but focused on looking at results and making changes when necessary.

Honoring language and ELP standards

With each school, language practice was a priority, stressed and supported throughout the day. In other words, ELs don't just go to ELD class, but are supported throughout the day. Secondary schools often have many priorities for instructional improvement, but placing an intense focus on language to the point that all teachers become language teachers, is rare in my experience. Schools might send some staff to be trained, but there is a difference between training some teachers and having a school focus on language consistently year after year. These three schools have this focus and their data is showing the growth.

Hiring and cultivating the right staff

It was interesting that each school focused so intently on hiring. As a seasoned administrator, I know the importance of making a quality hire, but I didn't realize how much time they put into not only hiring candidates who share their values, but also how much energy they invest into appreciating and celebrating their teachers. Building teacher leaders and creating a culture that celebrates and honors the work of teachers to ensure they are happy and remain, is a strong common theme at all three schools.

Protecting instructional time

I thought it was really interesting that all three schools volunteered how important it is to protect their teachers from becoming overwhelmed with too many initiatives. I would argue that taking on too many professional development initiatives, or not having enough focus or time to incorporate the learning, or doing something and then changing course two years later, is probably one of the most challenging aspects of being successful in teaching. It's simple: teachers need to know and be able to share in the vision. They need to be supported in their learning and they need to be able to focus over the span of years. They need time to become experts. Overwhelming teachers and changing course constantly is a recipe for disaster and a contributing factor as to why many veterans want to close their door and not welcome change. These administrators know this very well, and they take extra care to ensure their staff feel empowered and successful.

In my own experience as a teacher and as an administrator, I have seen groups read an article and change direction without thinking about its research base or the implications of implementation and sustainability. It is essential as your team embarks on creating a Blueprint that you design plans that have pedagogically sound and evidence based practices, and that your plans include details on how to implement effectively and sustain the efforts over time.

While the body of research relative to English learner success isn't as robust as one might wish it to be, we do have solid research on effective teaching practices for all children and the knowledge about effective learning practices and routines. The key here is making sure that the focus includes helping content teachers become language teachers and insisting on seeing growth and results in these areas.

Shared responsibility and collaboration

It was very evident in all three schools that ELD instruction was a shared responsibility where content, elective and ELD teachers work together to help ELs. Successfully educating English Learners and accomplishing equity – the idea that all students are reaching and exceeding standards – can only be done when the school as a whole understands the needs surrounding content learning and language acquisition for linguistically and culturally diverse students, and when all teachers embrace every child in their class as their own.

The passion for kids at these schools was palpable. ELs are valued members of the family and they make the efforts to ensure every child's needs are being met. They all have systems for supporting those students who require more academic and behavior supports and they go out of their way to celebrate them and challenge them too.

When I first became an ESOL Coordinator and toured the secondary schools in my district, the biggest concern that stood out for me was the fact that the responsibility for educating ELs was often viewed as being the responsibility of the ELD teachers in many cases. Other content teachers knew very little about what was being taught in the ELD class or how to support it. As a result, we made a concerted effort to share the standards for ELD across the schools, and change teacher perceptions regarding academic success and whose responsibility it lies with. These three schools do the same thing. They make sure ELP standards are included in core content classes and that teachers are thinking about how to reach all of their students.

It's difficult work, but the success for ELs depends on a collaborative approach wherein all adults in the school take responsibility and ownership for educating them.

Focus on the Individual Child

The longer I've been involved in EL education, the more I see the value and the academic success of ELs when efforts to improve their experience are focused on supporting the individual child, to the extent that is possible in schools with large EL populations. Designing cohesive plans centered on the student's emotional growth and confidence is just as important as the academic focus. If our goal is to ensure ALL students graduate on time and are prepared for college and/or career, we need to discuss what the word "all" means, and change or enhance our systems and our teaching to meet the needs of these children.

For example, what supports are necessary to ensure graduation is a reality, and where ELs and other disadvantaged youth are taking AP and IB courses, or receiving dual credit and seals of biliteracy? In schools with large populations of students living in poverty and where many are acquiring another language, being able to access the academic standards is really important, but so is attending to their social-emotional well-being. These are human beings - many of whom are struggling with life and don't really care about, or see the reason for doing a particular homework assignment. To ignore or not put resources into helping children navigate middle and high school is a missed opportunity.

With my Migrant Program Team, I have a counselor, a graduation coach, and several what we call migrant specialists, who are located at the schools. They work together as a team to identify students who are struggling and ensure they are having conversations with them, and are supporting them emotionally. They call home and make strong connections with parents over time. The migrant specialists help their students know what is needed for graduation and help them plan their courses each year; they help them fill out scholarships and FAFSA applications. This attention to relationship building and supporting students emotionally, and with their organization has made a significant difference.

It was heartening to hear that each school I interviewed practices the concept of Continuity of Care. They take the time to have adults looking after individual students. At the high school, it's about making sure they have the necessary support to graduate. At the K-8, it about making sure they are receiving the interventions, and are placed in the right classes and levels. At the elementary school, it's also about supports and interventions and making personal connections. In short, it's about relationships and making sure these kids don't go unnoticed.

Focused Professional Development for ELs and disadvantaged students

It may come across as overly simplistic, but teachers are very busy people who are working with many wonderful, young, needy human beings. It's a demanding, stressful job on a good day. To grow in their professional practice, teachers really benefit when they understand the big picture of what they are being asked to learn and why. They appreciate professional development that is focused and delivered over time; when it is engaging and practical, and when it helps them grow professionally. They appreciate time to plan and work with colleagues. They like to have the opportunity to give input and they don't appreciate it when they are asked to become experts in multiple initiatives in one year and stressed to the point of looking for another career.

That may be putting it simply, but it is amazing how many school districts don't respect or follow these simple guidelines. In my 20+ years as an educator, I have seen professional development initiatives come and go and teachers overloaded with so many priorities, that nothing is implemented well. Unfortunately, ELs often lose out in this process because they need teachers who understand how to make learning not only engaging and fun, but also accessible. This requires that they understand how to scaffold learning and plan with their needs in mind. It means that they need the time to learn and focus on how to support all of their students.

Professional development should be designed to focus on supporting all disadvantaged learners at its core - because good professional development will help all students - but if it's not designed with the EL, or students with disabilities, or children coming from poverty in mind as it's emphasis, then it runs the risk of becoming a 'sideshow' rather than the 'a main attraction,' or emphasis. We have so little time to learn as professionals, why are we not using that time to give teachers the tools to impact our neediest students?

Focus on effective classroom practices

A great deal of time and energy can be spent focusing on professional development that yields very little in terms of substantial growth in student outcomes. As educators, we know there are many ways to be effective practitioners, and yet we can sometimes spend too much time on initiatives that have us moving in too many directions or initiatives that don't really address the needs. For example, one district might decide that every class will teach writing in order to bring up scores across the district. This might be the yearly focus and all district trainings - the few that are offered - are focused on helping all core instruction teachers becoming writing instructors. While this may sound good and prudent to some, the details are more complex in implementing this initiative. For instance, what are the goals and how will you know when you've reached them? How will the instruction be differentiated to meet the needs of all learners? Will explicit methods be used to help support ELs? Who will make sense of a writing focus to PE and math teachers so that they understand why and how to incorporate it? Who will hold all teachers to growth and how will this be sustained and monitored over time? What do teachers feel about this and is there broad support? How is writing connected to reading and to speaking and listening and is anyone making those connections to teachers in the professional development offerings? Are the writing goals connected across grade levels? Is there a consistent approach? Finally, is anyone looking to see if this is in the best interest of students, and are English Learners advancing on their state exams and their language assessments?

These questions center around one example for professional development. However, having all teachers focused in one narrow aspect of instruction in this way without careful and thoughtful commitment to outcomes relative to all disadvantaged learners, can set the district back a long time when considering the fact that we don't have a great deal of time to get our disadvantaged learners to grade level and beyond.

When we have large populations of English Learners and children living in poverty, suffering from trauma and dealing with large gaps in education and exposure to high academic discourse, we may want to focus on district initiatives that get at those issues first, and then incorporate writing in a way that makes sense and accounts for differentiation.

With respect to English Learner success, I suggest that school and district teams identify outcomes for the year and focus on them; I suggest choosing several instructional practices that get at student engagement and meaningful interaction and that have the teacher becoming really good at being the facilitator of the knowledge rather than the expert; have high expectations and hold *all* students to the learning every day; have students routinely practice their language in meaningful ways that increase their use of academic conversations, and have them focused on critical reading and extending their knowledge into writing. Check to see if growth is happening regularly and adjust if not. Always be a learner and seek to improve when something doesn't go as planned. Dump the excuses.

No magic bullet exists and there is no one way of successfully teaching children, but there are in my experience, ways of helping ELs access the content. Using limited time and resources in a way that identifies key practices and has the potential for the greatest learning is the point.

Continuous Evaluation for Improvement

Organizations that want to continually grow and improve in a particular way need to cultivate a culture that is open to change. An organization that will be able to meet the challenges of changing student population must be able to adapt, rather than continuing to do things "because we've always done it that way." They need to provide a system for setting measurable and attainable goals that are timely and realistic and then have the means to evaluate its progress throughout the year. These evaluations then lead to revamping of program goals, beginning the cycle all over again.

Part of what really impressed me when I interviewed these schools, is that they are all focused on results. It's not enough to have goals and to look at data. It's about taking action and changing when the data shows students are not learning the standard. It's about coming together as a team and supporting one another. All three schools spoke about their teams and one even shared that when a teacher is not showing improvement, the data is out front for all to see, and the team, instead of being critical, steps up to offer support. Focusing on results is about developing a culture that believes in being the best they can be and striving to improve.

Core Value 3: Be Guided by Theory and Research

It's important to mention that theory and research are not the same thing. Research is a way of expanding our understanding on a certain topic based on repeated controlled tests to prove our ideas. In education we often like to move in a direction instructionally or programmatically when there is a body of research supporting moving in a particular direction. For example, there is a growing body of research that supports the success of English Learners in dual language programs.

When it comes to methods or programs to support English Learners outside of a dual language context, however, the research is not compelling.

Theory, by contrast, is more generalized thinking or a conclusion people have made based on an analysis. As you will read in the next section, *Being Grounded in the Law*, under the 9th circuit court case, *Castaneda v Picard*, English Learner programs must be based on sound educational theory.

The idea behind this core value is to plan and move in a direction that appears by experts in the field to be effective teaching practices for all children, while seen as essential for someone acquiring a new language. Be thoughtful and methodical. Read what studies exist and engage with researchers. Be planful and stay with your direction until you can observe if it is working or not working based on continually evaluating your data.

On the topic of researchers, I like visiting websites that compile all of the researchers in one place and sort them by their contributions. The website I like to visit is http://www.colorincolorado.org. They do a nice job of sorting and providing links to their articles.

Apart from visiting a website or database, however, I like to approach this topic in the classes I teach based on important contributors to the field of language acquisition strategies and supporting ELs in general.

For example, when it comes to gathering and synthesizing all of the current research on ELs providing clear concise information that helps EL Coordinators put together coherent programs, I choose Claude Goldenberg.

English Learner Research Synthesis & Summaries - Dr. Claude Goldenberg

Dr. Goldenberg is an authority on English Learner instruction and the author and co-author of several important articles that compile the research and provide guidance on what constitutes effective ELD and sheltered instruction. His work has influenced the way we approach our program delivery and what professional development and system-wide structures we put in place.

Two of the works I mention in this book are *Unlocking the Research on English Learners What We Know—and Don't Yet Know—about Effective Instruction* (2013) and, coauthored with Rhoda Coleman, *Promoting Academic Achievement Among English Learners: A Guide to the Research* (2010).

We collaborated with Dr. Goldenberg and a professor from the University of Oregon, Dr. Ilana Umansky, in creating a research based observational tool that would assess and inform our ESOL program's strengths and areas needing greater support. Two years later, we again collaborated with them to conduct a review of our K-12 ESOL and Bilingual programs.

Language Acquisition - Dr. Stephen Krashen

Comprehensible Input: Dr. Stephen Krashen, professor at the University of Southern California, and author of *Principles and Practice in Second Language Acquisition* (1982), is a pioneer in the field of second language acquisition and worth listing as a resource. He has made significant contributions relative to how people learn language and I find his theories around comprehensible input helpful and worth including as a foundational source. The idea that ELs acquire language in part, by understanding the essence of what is being said and having the level of language just above their ability. They then have to negotiate for meaning and that meaningful interaction process - when conditions are right - can lead to greater language growth and understanding. For teachers, this is why we talk about considering a student's background and the importance of using context and visual cues to help students understand the lesson.

Language Acquisition - Dr. Merrill Swain

Comprehensible Output: I have included Dr. Merrill Swain, professor emerita of second-language education at the Ontario Institute for Studies in Education, University of Ontario, due to her Output Hypothesis - a theory around language acquisition which states that learners of a language need comprehensible output as well as input. Many researchers feel that output is almost as important as input and that students need exposure to both. In my experience, I have watched structured student talk in small groups and observed students practicing their language use, negotiate for meaning and check for understanding. This does not happen naturally, of course. It's a process and establishing routines and teaching students how to have academic conversations is critical.

While Krashen has made important contributions, it is worth pointing out that his theories are not devoid of criticism. Furthermore, he disagrees with the output hypothesis arguing that comprehensible output is very rare, and it forces students to speak which raises their affective filter, thus making language acquisition more difficult. While this may be true in an unstructured setting, I have seen this to not be the case when done with purpose, and as I've stated above, many researchers would agree that comprehensible output is indeed important and helpful in learning a language.

Academic Language Development - Dr. Jeff Zwiers

Dr. Jeff Zwiers is a senior researcher at the Stanford Graduate School of Education. He has published articles and books on literacy, cognition, discourse, and academic language and is a great resource on how to structure comprehensible output - or having students interact in class using academic conversations. His book, *Academic Conversations: Classroom Talk That Fosters Critical Thinking and Content Understandings,* has been very instructive in my experience, helping teachers release the power and control of the classroom and allowing students to take a larger role in facilitating their own learning. Again, it's a process and involves practiced routines, but his work is spot on for leaders who are looking to focus on a few key practices to adopt and use as a focus.

Bilingualism and Biliteracy - Dr. Kathy Escamilla

I've included Dr. Kathy Escamilla, professor in the Division of Educational Equity and Cultural Diversity at the University of Colorado Boulder, due to her work related to the development of bilingualism and biliteracy for Spanish speaking elementary-aged students. Dr. Escamilla has been a friend and valued partner with Salem-Keizer School District over the years, as we have been a research district for her work with Literary Squared. Dr. Escamilla is well respected for her work on Spanish-English emerging bilingual children in U.S. schools and she promotes the use of one's native language to maintain a sense of identity, culture, and a great way to transition to English for English Learners.

Core Value 4: Being Grounded in the Law

Building Blocks: Federal Policy

Creating a blueprint for English learners involves the assessment and incorporation of key building blocks that serve as raw materials for a successful design. These blocks include basic policy (legislation and guidelines) from various levels in the educational hierarchy, including federal and state government, as well as district administration; and research that informs educational theory and best practices. Regarding ELs, there is a large body of literature to draw on to inform district policy.

Policy

While many parts of the EL blueprint creation process may be left to the district or individual instructors to decide, the federal government has laid out some clear policies and guidelines through legislation and court cases regarding the creation of an English learner educational vision. These government-mandated criteria should make up the foundation of your blueprint.

The federal government has progressively moved toward treating English learners with equity. In terms of education, *Linton & Davis, (2013), define equity* "Equity is not about equal treatment of students, but equal – and thus equitable – educational results. With equity, all students – no exceptions – are guaranteed success in school." (p. 19) They continue by saying, "… educational equity occurs when educators provide all students with the individual support they need to reach and exceed a common standard…. But educational equity can only be achieved in a school culture that supports this goal – not only for students, but for educators as well" (p. 19).

While the federal government's role in ensuring equity reaches the classroom is limited, there have been several important landmark court cases and laws that frame and propel our work in this regard. While I don't wish to get bogged down in citing pages of laws, I think it's important to build a common understanding as to why we offer ELD instruction and a few basics relative to the laws that govern our work. As such, I will be reviewing a few of the more pivotal court cases and laws passed that show this progression.

Fourteenth Amendment to the U.S. Constitution

The Fourteenth Amendment, adopted in 1868, declares that no state may deny any person the equal protection of the laws. This amendment protects the privileges of all citizens, provides equal protection under the law, and gives Congress the power to enforce this amendment through legislation.

This amendment is significant to because it takes the idea from the Declaration of Independence that all people are created equal, and puts it into the Constitution and gives it its soul. We are all equal citizens of this country and we have the same rights. (OPB, 2013)

Civil Rights Act

Following the death of President Kennedy, President Lyndon B. Johnson championed Kennedy's Civil Rights bill and signed it into law in 1964. This was the first major piece of legislation that addressed the idea of equity (Pub.L. 88-352, 78 Stat. 241). In it, the United States government prohibited discrimination based on sex, race, color, religion, or nationality and ended segregation of public places. The Civil Rights Act paved the way for future legislation related to equality and equity in education. (The Civil Rights Act of 1964, n.d.)

Lau v. Nichols

Probably the most significant court case related to the education of English learners was *Lau v. Nichols*, [414 U.S. 563 (1974)], a discrimination lawsuit brought against the San Francisco Unified School District in 1970. The lawsuit represented a Chinese student who was failing in school because he could not understand the lessons and was provided with no special assistance. The school district maintained that it provided the same instruction to all students and therefore was not discriminatory. In appeal, it made it to the Supreme Court in Lau v. Nichols, where the justices unanimously voted in favor of the plaintiffs in January 1974.

In his opinion, Justice William O. Douglas stated, "there is no equality of treatment merely by providing students with the same facilities, textbooks, teachers, and curriculum; for students who do not understand English are effectively foreclosed from any meaningful education."

The Court cited Title VI of the Civil Rights Act, noting that the students in question fall into the protected category established therein. (Lau v. Nichols, 2004-16)

Equal Educational Opportunities Act

The Equal Education Opportunities Act (EEOA) of 1974 [20 U.S.C. §1203(f)], prohibits states from denying equal educational opportunity to an individual on account of his or her race, color, sex, or national origin. The statute specifically prohibits states from denying equal educational opportunity by "the failure of an educational agency to take appropriate action to overcome language barriers that impede equal participation by its students in an instructional program." Unfortunately, this act introduced the vague and ambiguous phrase *appropriate action*, which would be better defined in Castaneda v. Pickard. (USDOE n.d.)

Castañeda v. Pickard

One of the other seminal post-Lau decisions concerning the education of English Learners was issued by the Fifth Circuit Court in June 1981. Castañeda v. Pickard (648 F2d 989 [5th Cir 1981]) was filed against the Raymondville, Texas Independent School District by Mexican-American parents who claimed that their children were being discriminated against due to their ethnicity. Although the Lau case established the need to provide additional support for ELs, it did not outline a way to evaluate the competence of the school's approach.

To support the idea set forth in *Lau* – that schools must take "appropriate action" for ELs – and to address the issue of segregation, the case established a three-pronged test, called the Castañeda standard to evaluate the adequacy of a district's program for EL students. Subsequently, the Castañeda standard has in essence become the law of the land in determining the basic adequacy of programs for ELLs.

In practice, I use the Castañeda standard constantly in planning and revising Salem-Keizer's ESOL Blueprint. In short, a program must be:

1. Based on a sound educational theory.
2. Implemented effectively with sufficient resources and personnel, and
3. Evaluated to determine whether they are effective in helping students overcome language barriers.

These guidelines have their shortcomings, however. Districts can appear to be following them and yet continue to underserve their ELs. Almost any program can be justified by an educational theory, and many students can be harmed after years of a district trying multiple approaches and discovering that they are ineffective. It's very important to design a program that not only follows the language of Castañeda, but the spirit of the ruling as well. Before deciding to use a new approach, it's important to look at the body of research to support it and consult experts in higher education to guide decision making. We want to avoid 'knee-jerk' decisions based on someone's idea or an article someone read. The ruling is about doing our due diligence in creating a program we strongly believe has the ability to transform the experience for our ELs. We will discuss the implementation of the Castaneda Standard in greater detail in chapter 2. (USDOE n.d.) (Write, W. 2015)

Plyer v Doe

The Texas legislature passed a law in 1975 which discouraged students who were not legally in the United States from attending public school and additionally withheld state funds from being spent on these children. A class action lawsuit was brought by families of Mexican origin on behalf of their children, claiming that they were unjustly being denied a free public education.

At issue - whether denying a free public education to undocumented children of illegal immigrants violates the Equal Protection Clause of the Fourteenth Amendment – was decided by the Supreme Court in favor of the plaintiffs by a 5-4 vote.

"The Court explained that 'education has a fundamental role in maintaining the fabric of our society' and 'provides the basic tools by which individuals might lead economically productive lives to the benefit of us all.'" (US Courts, Para. 5 n.d.)

Justice Blackmun wrote a concurring opinion stating, "When a state provides an education to some and denies it to others, it immediately and inevitably creates class distinctions of a type fundamentally inconsistent with "the purposes of the Equal Protection Clause because "an uneducated child is denied even the opportunity to achieve." When those children are members of an identifiable class, the state has created a separable and identifiable underclass. (U.S. Courts, Para 8, n.d.)

The Provision of an Equal Education Opportunity to Limited-English Proficient Students

The U.S. Department of Justice, Civil Rights Division and The U.S. Department of Education Office for Civil Rights (OCR) in *The Dear Colleague Letter re: English Learner Students and Limited English Proficient Parents (January 7, 2015)* has provided non formal general guidelines for districts to ensure that they meet the needs of English Learners, referred to in the guidance as Limited English Proficient students, or LEP. These guidance follow Castañeda, with Lau, and serves as the outline for Title III, Part A.

OCR does not provide specific details or requirements for what a program should look like or include, leaving these decisions up to the district. OCR does suggest taking the following steps to define "appropriate action":

- "identify students who need assistance;
- develop a program which, in the view of experts in the field, has a reasonable chance for success;
- ensure that necessary staff, curricular materials, and facilities are in place and used properly;

- develop appropriate evaluation standards, including program exit criteria, for measuring the progress of students; and
- assess the success of the program and modify it where needed." (USDOE, 2000)

Elementary Secondary Education Act

Part of President Johnson's "War on Poverty," the Elementary and Secondary Education Act (ESEA) became law on April 9, 1965. Its aim was to give all American children an education and therefore a chance at a good life, regardless of the income of their family of origin. (The Elementary and Secondary Education Act of 1965, n.d.) (Crawford, J. 2011)

Most relevant to this book are Title I and Title III. Title I provides funds to schools and other educational agencies with high percentages of low-income students:

...the Congress hereby declares it to be the policy of the United States to provide financial assistance... to local educational agencies serving areas with concentrations of children from low-income families to expand and improve their educational programs by various means (including preschool programs) which contribute to meeting the special educational needs of educationally deprived children. (Section 201, Elementary and Secondary School Act, 1965)

Title III of the ESEA, known officially as the English Language Acquisition, Language Enhancement, and Academic Achievement Act, provides funding for schools to enable students acquiring a second language to learn English and to meet academic standards expected of English speakers.

According to USDOE, (2012), the ESEA impacted future legislative action in several ways: 1) It specifically targeted economically disadvantaged children. 2) It provided aid directly to children in both public and private schools, rather than giving funds directly to the institution the recipients attended. 3) It gives states more power and vested interest in education. (California Department of Education, (n.d.)

No Child Left Behind

In the 1990s, there was a growing perception that America was losing its competitive edge to other countries. To address these concerns, the business community, along with Democrats and Republican lawmakers and Civil Rights groups, came together and updated the Elementary and Secondary Education Act. President George W. Bush signed the updated version, called No Child Left Behind (NCLB) into law on January 8, 2002. This bipartisan effort sought to boost the performance of schools in general, and close the achievement gap between poor and minority students and their more fortunate peers. The federal role in American education was increased and while states did not have to comply with the new requirements, they would risk losing federal Title I money if they did not.

Although this Act is considered extremely controversial with its prescriptive and unrealistic requirements, it did bring attention to the needs of English learners and held districts accountable to their success. (Klein, A. 2016a)

Every Student Succeeds Act

On December 10, 2015, President Obama signed an updated NCLB with the Every Student Succeeds Act (ESSA). The new act rescinds much of the large role the federal government had taken in education in NCLB, allowing states more authority for creating their own plans and policies. There are several sections that directly impact our work with ELs.

First, the act moves responsibility for English-language learners from Title III to Title I, making accountability for those students a priority. Second, once students have been in the country for more than a year, their reading and math test scores must be included in the rating for their school. In their third year and thereafter, their test scores must be considered the same as other students for proficiency accountability rating.

Schools that have populations with high dropout rates or struggling subgroups of students must work with their districts and states for intervention. (Klein, Alison 2016b)

Federal Guidelines for ELs: A summary

From these pieces of federal legislation, we see that districts are required to do the following for ELs: 1) avoid discriminatory practices, especially segregation (Civil Rights Act); 2) provide equal, not just identical, educational opportunities (Lau v Nichols); 3) avoid discriminatory practices against faculty, staff, and students (EEOA); 4) Use a three-part test to evaluate a state or district's EL Program (Castaneda v. Pickard) 5) Provide for the equal education opportunity to undocumented students acquiring a second language (Plyer v. Doe 6) To identify students who need help and ensure teachers have the resources and facilities to teach them effectively (USED OCR Provision) To specifically focus on economically disadvantaged children and ELs and provide the necessary supports (ESEA), 7) To account for growth and progress of ELs (NCLB & ESSA).

Core Value 5: Continuity of Care

The need for supports and interventions

So much of the dialogue in this country relative to education has focused on reaching standards, and testing. The federal government invested large sums of money and energy over the past decade with its efforts to bring up reading and math scores – accountable in high stakes testing – as the panacea for the problems in education. The premise being there is a problem in America's schools and we are going to fix it by holding districts and schools that receive title funding to a set of unrealistic goals. If they do not meet their goals, then they will be placed into improvement status and have to write improvement plans and perhaps incur other consequences. I have been a part of this system, both from the accountability side and the district compliance side. It has been a learning experience, to be sure.

Absent in this national 'dialogue' however, have been important factors that often plague English learners in our school systems: the profound effects of poverty and the changing demographics in America's schools—and their implications for instruction.

For example, according to the U.S. Census from 2014, the number of people living in poverty in America has grown to 46.7 million – higher than it's been since 1959. (DeNavas-Walt, C. & Proctor, B. , 2015) It's also important to note that the Hispanic population in this country reached a record 55 million in 2014. According to the census, the Hispanic poverty rate is at 23%, compared with the white poverty rate of 10%. (Krogstad, JM & Hugo Lopez, M (2015)

With the overall child poverty looming at 21%, it's important to understand how poverty and learning are related. ("Talk Poverty," n.d. pg 1) Impoverished children between 1-4 years of age are exposed to 13 million words - 32 million fewer words than their age peers from professional homes. So from the outset in kindergarten, students from poverty are behind in their exposure to words and pre-literacy skills (Hart, B., & Risley, T., Spring 2003)).

Students living in poverty will have more absences from school and will struggle with concentration and attention. They will have reduced cognitive abilities in many cases and a reduction in memory and creativity. (Jensen, 2009)

In addition, children from professional homes are given much more affirmation, which positively affects their self-esteem and leads to fewer behavioral issues. Children raised in poverty, however, often have inappropriate emotional responses, which often get them into trouble, often leading to discipline and self-esteem issues.

English learners, like other students, need supports and interventions to bolster their academic and personal growth. However, their cultural and socioeconomic backgrounds are often different from their native-English-speaking peers, which can create unintentional barriers and misunderstandings. Therefore, administrators need to take the need for cultural competence into account when devising the category of supports and interventions in the ESOL blueprint. It is essential to deal with these issues in ways that are progressive. So if your sub-group data show an achievement gap (e.g., your ELs are behind white native speakers in math), you must realize that we, the educators, own a significant part of the solution and are required to address these students where they are: in terms of the Core Values, we need to share responsibility and collaboratively focus on the individual child. Unless we do, large numbers of our students will continue to struggle and may be in danger of not being prepared for the ever-changing workforce of the 21st century.

Therefore, we need to focus on the individual child. Our job is helping young humans who are facing many struggles in our schools: self-concept, knowing where they fit in, poverty, low expectations from their family and their communities, language, teachers who don't understand the lens with which they view the world or their needs in terms of learning. They struggle in a system that was built for an industrial age – one that caters to white, middle class values. It addresses the importance of cultural competency, as well as examples of supports and interventions that ELs may find helpful.

Attending to Social-Emotional Needs

The concept behind Continuity of Care is just like the title suggests: it's about caring for long-term ELs in a systematic fashion. It's also about being intentional about the messages you are giving to the student and to their parents, messages about their value and worth to the school, to the district, and to our community. EL students need to feel accepted and loved like every other child. They need to feel that their background, experiences, beliefs, culture, are of equal value to that of the dominant culture. Parents too need to feel welcome to the school, respected and valued. They want to participate; it's just that they often do not know how.

We spend a lot of time discussing the need for all students to achieve a certain proficiency in reading and mathematics ability in this country but very little time on the whole child. Our ELs come to us with so many challenges, (as are all teenagers regardless of race, or economic status), but as long as they pass their state assessments, and make progress on their Annual Measurable Achievement Objectives (AMAO's), then we consider them to be okay. I disagree. Unless we attend to these students' self-concept in some fashion, we are neglecting a major component to their success. The challenges they face affect their self-esteem, their view of education, and their ability to integrate successfully into American culture.

Many of them do not have role models for going to college. Many live in poverty and some do not live in a culture that promotes higher education. In fact, for some girls in certain cultures, the emphasis placed on being a mother is much stronger than going to college or trade school. I remember working with a Hmong girl, for example, who was expected to get married at age 13. This particular girl did not, but she told me about others she knew who were secretly married since it's illegal to get married that young in this country. The stories are many and any teacher who works with ELs can tell you stories they have heard that speak to the challenges students face, some of which are tragic.

Most ELs are young impressionable human beings who need to feel supported emotionally as well as academically. Due to their challenging cultural difference, Salem-Keizer is working with each high school on providing Continuity of Care: additional adult mentoring and support for graduation and beyond. In addition to working with students, we host parent nights to build understanding and support for the ELD programs we offer and to seek their input.

What you choose to add in this category can look very different from what I've outlined below, but the point is that you are addressing a very necessary human component in addition to an academic one.

Sending Positive Messages

Addressing Continuity of Care is about the district and schools sending strong and consistent messages to ELs and their families that they are highly valued members of our community and our school community, which reflects the Core Value of an asset-oriented approach.

What messages are we sending our ELs? How are we building their self-esteem and encouraging them to be successful in the world? What messages are we sending them about their culture and language, traditions, and history, and working them into the narrative of the American experience? How are we setting them up to be our next generation of leaders?

Many of these kids are at-risk of dropping out or suffer from low self-esteem. They need to have the opportunity to share in their own success, and they need to hear from school and district officials that they are smart, capable individuals who have a bright future. What do we tell our ELs and their parents about their contributions, their worth, and their abilities to succeed?

In order to send them positive, encouraging messages about who they are and what they bring to our classrooms, schools, and society, we need to develop cultural competence and a school culture that provides more individualized support and attention to being on track to graduate, ensuring they are attending regularly, and that someone cares and is looking out for their future. We need to understand the challenges poverty brings and be able to address those in a comprehensive way. Moreover, as I mentioned earlier, we need to embrace cultural competency and continue on that path.

Encouraging Student Ownership in the Learning Process

I believe that students need to be partners in their own learning, and they have to want to succeed and strive to exit out of English Language Development (ELD) and to graduate. A tall order for some you say? Perhaps, but not unreasonable.

While we as educators are doing our part in making the curriculum engaging and the instruction interactive and meaningful, we also want our students to try their hardest. I have seen many extremely motivated EL students successfully exit the program in 4 or 5 years. In one case, a student was going to be placed at one of our Transition programs because he was at level 2, and all of our 1's and 2's attend one of two high schools, since we have so few at this level. His parents told him that he would take summer school and he would advance to level 3 on our language exam. Lo and behold, the student made it to level 3 and he was able to attend the high school of his and his parents choosing. I am not suggesting that a lack of student motivation is the reason for stagnation in all cases. What I am saying, is that it plays a role.

Knowing this, we brought all of our incoming 9th graders who have been in ELD for 5+ years, and their parents to a district meeting. At this meeting, all high schools had a team present to explain how they will be supporting the students, and my team and I gave a presentation about ELD – the purpose for it and how to exit. We wanted to set the expectation and let them know that we're here to help them, but that they too need to try their hardest to do their part.

Other ideas to consider are student-led conferences where students explain and show their parents what they've been working on and what they've achieved. Another is having the teacher log on to an online program where they can sign up their classes have their students upload speeches, Power Points, and other presentations. If planned carefully, teachers can work together with their peers and have the ELL students upload examples of their language achievements in all their classes, not just in ELD.

For ELs to be successful, they must share in the responsibility in their own learning and success.

Exiting ELD

For students wishing to exit ELD, they need to know the overarching landscape of their education and how ELD is designed to help them in all of their classes. If students take ELD but cannot answer why they are in there (It's a language support class to help them with the academic language they need to be successful in school) then we are possibly missing a key link to their success. If I as a student, I see that this class is different from my English class, and that it's helping me with the challenging language of my other classes, I might be more motivated and try harder both on a daily basis and in my summative language test.

Graduating

Perhaps more important than leaving ELD is obtaining a diploma and becoming a successful member of society. Students need to have a road map to graduation, be aware of how many credits they need in all subject areas to graduate, and know where they are in that process. For this reason, we created a graduation checklist and had students review the map we provide them during ELD class with their teacher once a semester. Students check off the credits they have earned in all the areas they need in order to graduate and look at where they are deficient. A sample graduation plan and checklist for Level 3 and 4 ELs in non-sheltered classrooms are included in the appendices C1-1.

Coaches and administrators can also use the checklist in talking with Long-term EL students (ELs who have been in the system for 5 years plus and are typically in grades 8-12) to help them avoid falling further behind and to give them ideas on how to make up credit deficiencies. For those who need to make up credits in summer school, we endeavor to have those discussions at these times.

Encouraging Parental Involvement

Parents need to know how to support their children in school and they need to receive the same messages their children receive– both in terms of how to graduate, why their child is in ELD and how they can exit, and that their child is special and deserving of a bright future. Bringing in the parents and explaining that you want to partner with them and their child shows respect and invites them into the school; an invitation that often needs to be overt, especially with some cultures or some individuals who may hesitate to enter a high school for various reasons, such as feeling uncomfortable or not feeling welcome; or having a lot of respect for the professionals at the school and not wanting to question their practices. Regardless of the many reasons for not wanting to participate actively, it is important to understand that all parents care about their child's education and they appreciate being informed and communicated with.

Salem-Keizer Parent Meetings

In my work with a district long-term EL workgroup I applied these ideas that students need to be partners in their own success, and parent (or guardian) involvement needs to be high, especially as they enter high school. Parents/guardians play a key role in supporting teachers and their child. Parent support is really important as students transition into high school in 9th grade, but at this juncture we actually see many parents taking less of an active role.

Keeping this in mind, my team and I set up a series of district meetings, the first of which included representatives from each high school. Our goal was to include every incoming 9th grade long-term EL student (most of whom had been in ELD since first grade) and their parent(s) to one of the high schools, where we provided dinner, and childcare. My team and I gave the main presentation in which we addressed why students are in ELD and how the class is designed to support them, and then we broke them up into groups according to which high school their child will be attending. In my talk, I explained how students exit the program and essentially tried to create partners in the work. We stressed the importance of trying hard on the ELPA21 (our state's summative language assessment), and good attendance. We explained to them what they can expect from an ELD class and told them about the graduation requirements. We created a graduation check sheet and provided one to each family. Following the meeting, we set up additional meetings for the parents and students who did not attend.

By building awareness, it was our hope to get a few more to try a little harder to succeed. We thought that if we build partnerships and build awareness with parents and students and if we provide more adult care and guidance, we might really begin to show a shift in our data. Even if we are still not as successful as we'd like to see, we're still being very proactive and focused, which can't be bad.

Pilot Project: Emotional Support for Long Term ELs

As an outcome of the Long-term EL Workgroup I formed in Salem, administrators from each high school decided to start a pilot program that sought to support a small group of ELs emotionally throughout the year, the theory being that students perform better and are more engaged with school when adults are spending individual time with them and showing that they care about their success. The workgroup consisted of assistant principals from each high school, the lead counselor for the district, and English Language Acquisition Specialists who are specialized instructional coaches. Our work on the pilot project consisted of three distinct phases: planning, implementation and evaluation.

Planning

We selected 10 incoming 9th grade EL students who had been in ELD for 5+ years. Each school decided on the criteria they would use to choose students from that group. Some chose students who were attending regularly but seemed to be struggling emotionally. Others looked at credits for graduation and chose to focus on making sure the student was on track to pass his classes and knew what he needed to graduate.

We also identified adults at the school who would be assigned to one of the students. The criteria for choosing adults varied from school to school, but basically, the discussion involved choosing teachers who already knew and worked with the students and who expressed an interest in doing this work. Schools assigned students to this adult (typically one of their teachers), and it was expected that this adult would check in with the student monthly.

We asked each school to create a sustainable plan and shared their plans at one of our Long-term EL (LTEL) meetings. My goal in this was to have the schools develop their own structure – one that suited their culture and their needs. Therefore, the pilot project looked different at each school. While the plans differed, most of them had more than one adult checking in with each child periodically so that he or she would feel that a lot of people were concerned and looking out for their success. Plans often included the following:

- Students meet periodically as needed with the community outreach specialist or Migrant Specialist (classified personnel who currently support EL students and families).
- Licensed Teachers analyze assessment data from mainstream classes and communicate with LTELs and parents about achievement. Contact is logged.

- Administrators identify freshmen LTELs with multiple failing grades and low GPA for one-on-one conversations and log contact.
- Assistant Principal, English Language Acquisition Specialist, or an ELD teacher periodically review data and conference to monitor progress of LTEL students.
- Team meets quarterly to discuss students and make plans for ongoing support.

Implementation

As the first phase of implementing our Continuity of Care program, we contacted the students we had chosen and discussed the program with them.

Then the students met with the adults on multiple occasions during the year, reviewing their graduation progress, their grades, offering support and showing that they cared. The teachers keeping record of students' progress during this time.

Evaluation

To determine if the program was successful and where it needed improving, we had the ELAS or EL Facilitator record the anecdotal evidence and other data in the early spring and bring it to our LTEL Workgroup, where we would discuss the value of the program, and what changes, if any needed, to be made. The team convened to analyze the data and make decisions about year two. We focused on refining this process to include more students, to continue with the existing students, and to make the process easy to manage. Although we didn't have quantitative data to show how this project worked, we did have ample anecdotal data from administrators, coaches, and teachers who said that the work was valuable and had positive effects.

We found that our added focus on these students who need the support through a Continuity of Care pilot project was difficult to create, facilitate, and sustain. This was especially the case in schools with large EL populations, because setting up systems where adults essentially mentor students takes time and energy – energy that is often hard to sustain when teachers are already maxed out with teaching and extra duties. That said, however, it's one idea that may pay dividends with some of your most struggling EL students.

In summation, supports and interventions can take many forms. The above examples are merely to provoke thought and create ideas of your own. The essence of putting this blueprint category into place, however, is to bring in the human element and address the emotional needs of children who are struggling. They need our very best effort. They need attention and great instruction. They need a system that promotes continuity of care.

ACTIVITIES: Creating a list of your own core values and overarching goals

The first activity for this chapter is to come up with a set of your own core values and create several overarching goals, which will guide your work. Ideally as a group, getting clear on what you believe will serve as a foundation for building your ELE Blueprint. From this work you may decide to develop a mission statement or a set of guiding questions that can help articulate your plans to various stakeholders. Feel free to borrow the core values listed in the book, or choose your own. Perhaps you only want to have a robust discussion with a leadership team and form some agreements. Regardless, the activity below is one strategy my team and I use when working with teachers to generate discussion or when we show them how to work with EL students and get them talking.

Give One/Get One

Procedure:

Have each member of the group fold a piece of paper in half.

Give them a few minutes to generate multiple ideas based on the essential questions asked, and write them in the left hand column of the paper.

Have each member of the group get up and circulate around the room, pair up and share – "Give One" idea each.

Participants write down the new idea they received on their paper in the right hand column along with the partner's name.

Repeat as desired (Three times is usually enough).

Brainstorming Charts

Core Value Brainstorm	Overarching Goals Brainstorm

The second group activity is to take your overarching goals and create a mission statement and/or a set of guiding questions to be shared with your stakeholders. You may choose to have a smaller group work on this and bring it to the larger group at a following meeting. Or, perhaps you naturally take the above brainstorm and complete this activity in one setting.

Mission Statement and/or Set of Guiding Questions Brainstorm

CHAPTER 2

Creating a Blueprint for Change

Chapter Objective:

- To understand what an ELE Blueprint is and how develop one.
- To create the overarching categories for your district's ELE Blueprint, and provide areas of focus under each category that represent the initial phase of implementation.

Getting Started

Defining the ELE Blueprint

In architectural language, a blueprint is detailed technical document that maps out the plans for a structure such as a house. It contains measurements, schematics, views from different sides, labels of different elements, lists of materials, and other important information necessary for constructing a dwelling.

Likewise, a district's ELE Blueprint is the primary vision document that guides all district staff forward over a span of years. At minimum, a blueprint will contain a set of overarching categories, such as Curriculum and Instruction, under which all goals and focused work will be outlined in phases. It should also provide the research base for the work.

I also recommend including a list of ESOL terms and a set of core values spelled out as well because personnel change and newcomers will benefit from reading the document and understanding how and why the work was created. Additionally, teachers will benefit from knowing and participating in the discussion around core values.

The blueprint is a living document that changes and evolves over time for all who work with English Learners. For Upper management and the school board, it is a plan for closing the achievement gap: they can use it to request reports and progress updates. Administrators use it for goal setting with their staff in terms of achieving equity, observing classrooms, and evaluating teachers. Teachers benefit from knowing there is a well-articulated plan in place for ELs, that the district supports this work and what their role is in supporting the overall goals.

Blueprints are intended to be an organic process for each district therefore; it will look different from place to place. Who decides what will be included in the blueprint will also look different in each district, but it should be an inclusive process so that all feel they have voice in what needs to happen for EL success.

The Importance of Having an ELE Plan

While there is no single formula that can solve the challenges involved in educating English learners, there are steps a district can take to create a successful blueprint to achieve success.

It's important that these steps be implemented in a way that is targeted and focused on EL growth and achievement. I cannot stress enough that ELs and other disadvantaged students must be at the center of all district planning. (I have included a sample program management-planning template and an example in the appendices C2.1)

In addition to making ELs the priority, we must exercise the Core Values of being committed to our plan and open to continuous improvement and evaluation. We must use the building blocks of research and best practices to make sure our students have a system that is aligned and prepared for their success.

Because every district is in a different situation, not every idea or process identified in this book will work for everyone. The power, however, in having a district secondary leadership team read this book together, is the rich discussions related to customization and differentiation that will ensue. The more discussions focusing on the needs of English learners that occur across an entire leadership team in a district, the more chance ELs have at succeeding in school.

There are many challenges associated with implementing large-scale initiatives, and institution wide change, especially from a central office, must be carefully planned and monitored to ensure success. Therefore, it is essential to establish an understanding around the need for change and get the majority of staff to know, articulate, and support the vision. All players need to see themselves in the vision, understand the direction the district is taking and feel empowered to teach and give input. This requires strong communication, a well-articulated plan founded in achievement data, guided by research and implemented in phases.

Understanding that a process is required to effectively design and implement such a plan, I have outlined the steps necessary for laying a foundation to building your ELE 'house.'

Select an ELE Blueprint Committee

The ELE blueprint committee will work together to set goals for your ESOL program. This team should be made up of those who will ultimately support and promote the program within the district and encourage others to follow the vision. Choose people on your committee who represent all levels of the blueprint, but the structure of that committee can look very different depending on the district.

One option would be to have a single committee that includes top district decision makers (e.g., superintendent, assistant superintendent, curriculum directors, HR and finance directors), and include the ESOL coordinator and several principals. If structured this way, the ESOL coordinator will have to lead the work in getting feedback from various groups and perhaps collaborate with the assistant superintendent (or someone who leads the district in some capacity) in messaging the goals for the work and how input will be gathered.

Another approach is to divide the work into three groups: 1) a leadership team that makes decisions, made up of the players mentioned above; 2) an advisory committee that responds to the leadership teams questions (e.g. teachers, support staff, parents, students, instructional coaches); and 3) community groups that serve to provide input (e.g., parents, students, teachers, principals).

Another option is to have one large committee that includes voices representing all aspects of the blueprint. For example, one would want all top district decision makers as well the ESOL Coordinator, an instructional coach perhaps, an ELD teacher perhaps, and a parent and or student.

There may be other ways to set up teams that aren't represented here, which is great. Keep in mind as you do this, however, that transparency is key to success. If important stakeholders feel like they don't have a voice in the new direction, then any change is going to be that much harder.

Important stakeholders include the following:

- *Superintendent:* Whether or not the superintendent sits on the committee will vary from district to district. The important point is that the superintendent is visible in the beginning, sets the tone for the task ahead, and lays out his or her expectations of the committee.

The superintendent is also the primary communicator to the School Board and to the community, and can address the work that is taking place related to equity and ensuring that plans are being made to ensure all learners are reaching and exceeding the standards and benchmarks.

- *Assistant Superintendent:* The Assistant Superintendent should ideally lead or be directly involved in the committee. He or she may lead the in establishing group norms (agreed-upon behaviors), facilitate the discussion and ensure the committee is moving forward in a positive way. He or she will act as a group spokesperson to the superintendent, the district's secondary principals, and the larger community, establishing the tone and expectations.

- *Grade-Level Directors:* Individuals who lead the principals at given levels should have a definitive voice and be present in the discussions, which links the ELE blueprint building process to current issues in classrooms, rather than treating it as a separate silo. This work needs to be seen as central to the success of all students, and therefore grade-level directors should be present.

- *Curriculum Directors:* It is important to include in the blueprint planning process those who make choices about instructional materials. In this way, the ELE blueprint will be directly connected to the learning materials used in the district's classrooms.

- *Principals:* A sampling of secondary principals should be present. It's important to have the voice of those leading the change in schools to have a voice at the table – to read the research, and share in the exciting dialogue of setting a vision.

- *ESOL Director/Coordinator:* The person responsible for the ESOL Program in the district is the key participant. He/she is responsible for finding and submitting research to the committee, conducting listening sessions, and distributing surveys. He/she collects the data and analyzes it for the group. This person would most likely facilitate many of the discussions and work closely with the Assistant Superintendent and or the Curriculum Director in the planning and running of the meetings. This person is also responsible for secretarial duties (or assigning someone): creating agendas, sending out meeting reminders, taking minutes, sending out notes after each meeting, etc.

- *Program Assistants/Teachers on Special Assignment/ Instructional Coaches:* If instructional coaches are employed by the district, I recommend including them in the discussion. Coaches, especially ones with experience teaching ELs and observing classrooms across the district, can be very informative as to the current conditions across district schools.

It's important to remember that communicating with these people and seeking their feedback is a vital part of the process. Even if they were unable to attend the planning sessions, you can still keep them informed throughout the process.

Meetings should be monthly and the goal should be to build a vision over the span of a school year, with the idea of implementing the following year.

Establishing Positive Group Dynamics and Norms

As with many groups, it's important to establish norms, or agreed upon behaviors so that people feel heard and respected. A great deal of passion can be generated around this issue, and it's important to set a tone of professionalism, active listening and valuing others for their ideas and concerns. This will help establish a basis for the idea behind Shared Responsibility and Collaboration within the Focused, Intentional, and Results Oriented Core Value. While group norming needs to be organic and derive from each group, I strongly encourage including drafting an agreement that includes language that speaks to the values listed below:

1. Set clear outcomes for each meeting and remain focused on the task
2. Believe that all students are able to learn at high levels
3. Commit to focusing on solutions rather than challenges

4. Establish a safe zone where participants feel safe to speak openly without fear of judgment or retribution, and where opinions are kept confidential.

The Castañeda Standard

In building a blueprint for Salem-Keizer, I referred to the Castañeda Standard to help guide my work and establish a strong foundation that would align with the goals and requirements of state and federal law. As mentioned in Chapter 1, the three criteria of the Castañeda Standard require that programs for ELs are 1) pedagogical soundness, 2) effective implementation, and 3) demonstrable results. In thinking about this standard, English Language Development (ELD) is as much about the system as it is the instruction. All pieces have to be working together. Achieving success requires strong communication across the district and good systems of support, dynamic instruction, and strong vision leadership. When one of the links is either missing or weak, the whole system can suffer as a result, slowing down progress. In your blueprint, it is important to design it in a way that ensures all elements are working in concert.

Keeping the Castañeda Standard in mind, I set out to build a vision document that would purposefully move our ELE Program in a powerful direction. I wanted to purposefully address the challenge of educating ELs to ensure their ultimate success in school and in life, in a way that was purposeful, focused, intentional, and connected.

The Design: Categories for Improvement

From these Castañeda building blocks, and your established core values, you'll create a design of your choosing based on your district's individual needs.

When I first took my position at Salem-Keizer as ESOL coordinator, I was fortunate in that a group of districts had gathered to discuss and focus on EL success. As part of their process, the group had created a rubric, identifying eight priorities and a list of descriptors one would hope to find in a comprehensive program for ELs, which would act as benchmarks for determining progress. The eight priorities were 1) leadership, 2) planning, 3) literacy, 4) interventions, 5) collaboration, 6) rigorous academics, 7) English development, and 8) assessment.

While their rubric had meaning overall, its downfall was that each priority had too many descriptors—in fact, there were over 100 descriptors schools were supposed to rate themselves on and look to improve upon. To my way of thinking, this wasn't very practical for building focus or momentum. Not surprisingly, the rubric never really produced any serious or sustained traction anywhere in the state.

My own experience showed that sheer number of descriptors was too overwhelming and had little chance for being implemented with fidelity across the years. But I liked the concept of the big categories, and I liked the focus it had the potential to provide. So, taking this rubric, and looking at the needs of my district after completing my own evaluation process, I adapted their list and as a team we created the categories that would later become our own *ESOL Blueprint for Success*. Within each of the categories, we also added Essential Questions that helped guide and inform our thinking, as well as goals and tasks to help us determine if progress had been made.

My final list of categories represented all of the major ones in the rubric mentioned above, with a few changes: I combined some of the components and altered the names. For example, I am an ardent supporter of Rigorous Academics for ELs, but I included that component into 'Supporting Quality Instruction.'

Based on your district's needs, I strongly encourage you to create your own categories. If you are not fortunate enough to have a group that has thought through what specific areas need to be addressed, you can determine your categories by discussing issues with key stakeholders.

Introducing the Salem-Keizer Blueprint

I built the frame of our plan rooted in research, looked at our data, at our instruction, at our system, and after consulting with others, made a vision document that is, to our way of thinking, straight-forward and manageable.

The approach we took at Salem-Keizer proved to be particularly fruitful. After one of our program reviews, conducted by Claude Goldenberg of Stanford University, teachers, administrators, and coaches all spoke to their being a vision and that we are moving along on a good path, especially considering where we had been prior to this process. While not perfect, staff can see that we are moving forward with purpose, and that is powerful!

Salem Keizer's Blueprint Categories

The box below lists the broad categories of the Salem-Keizer blueprint for secondary schools. I have added brief descriptions below for each one to serve as an example for how we structured our work. You can view the full blueprint and rubric in the appendices C2.2 & C2.3

SALEM-KEIZER ESOL BLUEPRINT

CATEGORIES
- LEADERSHIP
- SUPPORTING QUALITY INSTRUCTION
- STANDARDS AND CURRICULUM
- SUPPORTS AND INTERVENTIONS
- ACCOUNTABILITY: EVALUATION & ASSESSMENT

Leadership

Regarding leadership, we at Salem-Keizer have been focusing on four key areas. First, all administrators should know the vision for ELs in the district and feel like they can have input into its direction. To this end, communication about all aspects of the blueprint as it relates to their school and professional development and coaching support for their teachers is discussed. Second, leadership should discuss with each school their professional development needs regarding ELs and other disadvantaged students. Third, administration should run data and determined how each high school can best support their long-term ELs, meeting quarterly as a workgroup to discuss. Fourth, as a staff of coaches, we are building the ideas around equity into all of our trainings and providing schools with a common definition of *equity* and with building cultural Awareness and Competency.

Regarding leadership, we at Salem-Keizer have been focusing on four key areas. First, all administrators should know the vision for ELs in the district and feel like they can have input into its direction. To this end, communication about all aspects of the blueprint as it relates to their school and professional development and coaching support for their teachers is discussed. Second, leadership should discuss with each school their professional development needs regarding ELs and other disadvantaged students. Third, administration should run data and determine how each high school can best support their long-term ELs, meeting quarterly as a workgroup to discuss. Fourth, as a staff of coaches, we are building the ideas around equity into all of our trainings and providing schools with a common definition of *equity* and with building cultural awareness and competency.

Supporting quality instruction

If our primary goal is to build instructional capacity at every grade level and in every core subject area, we need to support that objective in tangible ways. Some of the methods we've used in Salem-Keizer to support students in their learning involve establishing instructional routines that support productive classroom habits. We also require ELs to be speaking and using high academic vocabulary in all of their classes throughout the day, as well as supporting teachers and allowing them to do the best they can, by investing in instructional coaches who specialize in ELD and SIOP. These coaches provide professional development and work with teachers individually throughout the year. All ELD teachers meet in district-wide professional learning communities several times a year to plan together and learn from each other. Supporting ELD teachers across the district in this way has greatly improved the understanding and use of ELP standards, the use of quality ELD resources, and quality unit planning with colleagues and coaches.

Standards and curriculum

For Salem-Keizer, it was important that teachers be aware of the English language proficiency standards and how they were related to the Common Core Standards. We invested a lot of time deconstructing and introducing the new ELP standards to all of our teachers and coming up with common agreements about what standards to emphasize at certain points. We also spent a year piloting highly engaging instructional materials – materials teachers, parents, and students are excited about. Note that Standards and Curriculum are two separate categories in the Salem-Keizer Blueprint; for sake of space, we have chosen to combine them in the book. Also note that the standards in your particular state may be different.

Supports and interventions

Salem-Keizer offers a number of instructional supports and interventions for students all day every day. By educating staff about their students' languages, cultural differences, and challenges, we've developed an environment of cultural competency, where students feel welcome and safe, regardless of home language and national origin. Our instructors also focus on positive messaging, and we are also working with each high school on providing what we term Continuity of Care for certain students: we provide additional adult mentoring and support for graduation. In addition, we share important information with students (and their parents) to help them partner with us in their own learning process.

Accountability, evaluation, and assessment

Salem-Keizer expresses its commitment to the Core Value of being Focused, Intentional and Results Oriented, by holding its program accountable to periodic evaluation. We recognize the importance of collecting data and including reviews by our teachers, administrators, and third parties. Our administrators play an important role in assessing how teachers, students, and the program overall are faring. We also contracted with experts in the field of EL education to provide a Program Review and a data review of our ESOL/Dual Language programs.

ACTIVITY 1: Creating Overarching Blueprint Categories

In the previous chapter, you have read about and discussed a set of core values that now guide your work in a purposeful way. Being clear from the start on what you believe and why you are embarking on this journey is a healthy, essential first step. The next step - and goal of this chapter - is to determine the major blueprint categories for your district, and decide on some areas from which to focus.

The strategy listed below is an example of a group protocol designed to make people think about an essential question, brainstorm ideas and share them in a safe, collaborative manner. You may have your own process for the same purpose, but the point is that your group defines the work and categorizes it in some fashion. The list you create will ultimately evolve over time and will change as you go through getting input from all of your stakeholders, but it will be a good place to begin the planning process. My only warning is to not create a list of priorities that is so large that implementing it sounds good, but is in fact, unrealistic. Think in terms of creating several categories and eventually making a 3-5 year plan of implementation.

Numbered Heads Together

Procedure:

Divide the committee into groups of three or four.

Give each person in the group a number from 1-4

Pose an essential question/s to the group.

Have the group discuss the essential question/s, make sure everyone in the group understands and can answer.

Repeat the question and call out a number randomly.

Group members with that number stand up and when called on, answers for the team.

Your Ideas/brainstorm	Draft Categories
Discussion Notes - Main Ideas	Final Categories

ACTIVITY 2: Creating a Leadership Structure

In this activity, you will create a leadership structure that works for your district. This activity involves a group dialogue that will determine roles and responsibilities. The boxes below are only suggested templates to help your thinking. If you have another way of organizing your structure, that's great too.

Cabinet Leadership Team: This will be the decision-making body

Suggested participants -

- Superintendent
- Assistant Superintendent
- Other cabinet members representing other aspects of the district (transportation, technology, etc.)
- Curriculum Directors, High School Directors, Elementary Directors

Leadership Committee: This will be a district advisory group that will listen, observe, research, and make recommendations to the Cabinet Leadership Team.

Suggested participants -

- Assistant Superintendent
- Other cabinet members representing other aspects of the district (transportation, technology, etc.)
- Curriculum Directors, High School Directors, Elementary Directors
- Central Office Administrators (ESOL Director/coordinator, etc.)
- Principals

Advisory Committee: This will be a key group of people who will learn about your programs and provide feedback and suggestions for improvement.

Suggested participants -

- School Board members
- Community partners
- School staff who work with families
- Parents representing different language groups - ensuring all major languages are represented in the group.
- Members of the leadership committee

Now that you have your key stakeholders, it will be important to identify a point person who will be responsible for scheduling meetings throughout the year, arranging child care, interpreters, providing agendas, etc.

CHAPTER 3

Seeking Input and Communicating Key Data

Chapter Objectives:

- To discuss ways to include a variety of voices in the design of your blueprint.
- To discuss the importance of being data-driven and creating a data team that focuses in part on creating and telling EL Data stories.

In this chapter, I will discuss how you can determine and communicate the needs of different groups that are part of our ELE program. We will discuss how gather information on the perspectives of various groups and discuss how to communicate those stories in a way that is effective and compelling.

Seeking Input

When going through a program realignment process and creating a blueprint for the coming years, it is essential to listen to all voices of those who are close to ELs to inform your ELE plan. Leading a district through difficult systemic change will require that you know your current data on ELs, what other groups feel about your current system, and where you need to focus instructionally and systematically. This process is time consuming, but it's important. I spent the first two years altering systems and understanding where I needed to go before really crafting a clear vision document. With that being said, don't feel that it's going to take years before you can begin facilitating discussions. In truth, we are building vision and tweaking systems simultaneously. To the extent that you can take the time to seek input from important group ahead of time, however, you will be further ahead and more able to answer questions and facilitate productive discussions.

You need to understand what various groups in your district and in your community feel about what is working and what is not working in your system. It's necessary to actively listen and to be open and as transparent as possible throughout the process, which embodies the Core Value of being Focused and Intentional and Results Oriented - Openness to Continuous Evaluation and Improvement. One of the easiest ways to listen the input of others is through focus groups.

Choosing your interviewees

It is important to create focus groups whom you may survey and, or bring together over a series of dates to discuss items and gain their feedback. When you interact in this way with different groups who interact with ELs, you learn information from various perspectives. Your respondents may even offer helpful ideas for resolving the issues you are facing! My advice is to listen to and survey as many groups as you can, analyze the data, and observe classrooms across the district's schools – both ELD and content – so that when your team is ready to discuss focus areas for a Blueprint, you will have a solid understanding of your strengths and areas needing improvement; and, you will have data in hand to inform your decisions. The groups I have found important to include are the following:

Teacher Groups

It's ironic, but often when we discuss reform in education, we often forget to listen to the practitioner's – professional teachers who work with students, day–in-and-day-out. In this case, we need the input of ELD teachers. Their voices are essential to understanding the challenges and the reality of situation you are facing. That being said, a simple dose of caution is in order, because while their contributions are important in understanding the whole picture, occasionally, some teachers may mistakenly operate under false assumptions or beliefs (e.g., "ELs can't function in regular core content classrooms") or their idea of rigor might be vastly below what it needs to be. Sometimes it's easy to fall into the trap of not being able to see past daily challenges or blaming the lack of student growth on personal anecdotes and perceptions, rather using data and research as a guide. Regardless of the teachers' perceptions, you can learn a lot about the situation you face – both in terms of the challenges your students and your teachers face, and the obstacles you have to address with your teaching staff in terms of separating myth from fact.

During our program reviews in Salem-Keizer, we pulled focus groups of teachers together to get their opinions. We then partnered with Education Northwest, an education laboratory, to create a survey to be given each year to our teachers. We spent a great deal of time identifying the types of information we wanted them to comment on so that our evaluation process could address the areas we found needing improvement.

Instructional Coaches

If you are fortunate enough to have a cadre of instructional coaches, or even better – coaches who specialize in language acquisition – then seeking their input can be extremely important. Not only do they see the district from a much broader programmatic perspective, they also have connections with teachers, have taught themselves, and can pinpoint and articulate the strengths and weaknesses.

If you do not have a cadre of experts, perhaps you have a district specialist or teacher on special assignment (TOSA; a teacher who leaves the classroom to perform other duties for a limited time) or you can reach out to other regional educational support systems, such as regional education service districts (ESDs), or a local education laboratory, for personnel to contribute to your focus group.

In Salem-Keizer, we imbedded in a core group of instructional coaches into the high schools since we found the needs for support were so great. Their work of coaching ELD teachers and providing ongoing professional development - ensuring all PD included EL supports - made a significant difference as we learned through as series of focus groups of teachers and administrators, and through survey results. Including their voices in this blueprint design process was extremely valuable in a number of ways.

Regardless of whether or not you have instructional coaches, having language acquisition experts come together to help advise and instruct your plans can be truly rewarding and beneficial to moving ahead and reinforces the idea of Shared Responsibility and Collaboration in Core Value 2.

Parent Groups

Title IA and Title IC require districts to include parents in the design and implementation of your programs, in groups called Parent Advisory Committees (PAC). This is a great place to begin communicating with parents and seeking their input. You might have them take a brief survey or gather them into small groups to express their thoughts and opinions about their children's experience in school. I always find in working with adults (students too) that setting up the conversation in small groups, and showcasing their ideas in some way is always more productive than asking the whole group what they think. Parents feel engaged and valued and often share their experiences with their neighbors, which can increase your attendance in future meetings.

Talking with this group may be enough for you to move forward with creating your blueprint, and then again, it may not. You might consider working with one or two of your schools with already established parent groups representing second language learners, and organizing separate meetings using a similar approach. Explain that you want to know how they feel about their child's education, and if they have suggestions for improvement.

In my travels around the state visiting with multiple EL parent groups, I found that many districts met with parents largely to provide information about the school or about Title I. They didn't reach out to this group with the sole purpose of listening and learning. Parents (including those who primarily speak a language other than English) really appreciate it when they are asked for their opinions.

Community Groups

What groups in your community represent or assist your minority populations? Are there organizations helping your migrant community? Do community colleges in your area have programs designed to help migrant students or other minority groups?

Building partnerships with these organizations and listening to their experiences and their ideas not only helps inform your work, this asset-oriented approach also builds trust and provides potential in-roads to community leaders and others who will help you along the way.

It's worth mentioning that some community advocacy groups have an agenda and may want to provide regular' guidance,' or insist certain elements are included in your plan, which may or may not make sound educational sense. Remember that your goal is to listen and learn and to foster relationships; by establishing clear objectives from the beginning (and perhaps talking with your superintendent ahead-of-time), you can avoid misunderstandings and keep the relationship intact.

In addition to Parent Advisory Committees mentioned in the preceding section, in Salem-Keizer we formed an advisory committee that involved over 20 members of staff, community members and parents. This group met several times throughout the year and provided valuable input, and helped steer the decision making process of our English Learner programs. I explain this process in more detail in chapter 7.

Student Groups

Finally, it is vital to know how students are feeling about their classes and their overall education. Done in a controlled, safe way, students will be more than happy to give their opinions. I remember going around the state and meeting with student groups at high schools, asking about their experiences, and thinking how rich I was for having done so. When students tell you how bored they are, or how they don't feel smart, or how a teacher goes too fast and doesn't explain things well, you get a strong grasp of what they are experiencing and how they are viewing the world.

I believe in being very open and honest with high school students. I like to explain that we (the district) believe in their success and we want to make sure they have everything they need to achieve and graduate. I typically explain that the data is showing that many are not doing very well, and ask them if they can speak to why they think that is. You will get a sense very quickly as to what they think, and often they can pinpoint exactly what isn't working for them in the classroom.

In the survey we created with Education NW, we also created one for students, and provided it to all middle and high school students to gain their voice in the ongoing development of our program. This was very successful and the input helped ground our work.

Incidentally, sharing this information with the principal and/or district leadership can be very powerful in terms of moving change forward. If for example, students talk about the fact that teachers are talking too fast or don't explain things well, moving ahead with implementing common sheltered strategies across the school, might be seen as a crucial next step.

Conducting Focus Groups

I have been involved in developing different ways to set up focus groups. Most recently, we (the organizers of the meetings) divided the district into regions and brought school personnel (consisting of an administrator, a coach, a couple teachers from each school in that region) and parents and students together to learn about the various programs we offer, outline some of our challenges, and seek their input. We captured input by surveying the groups in several ways at those meetings:

1) We posted questions on a screen and had participants respond electronically using clickers.

2) We had table groups and had them discuss questions and write down their thoughts and questions on paper.

3) We had participants divide into interest groups (those who wanted to participate in a bilingual programs discussion and an ESOL discussion for example), and provide answers to two essential questions related to program improvement on chart paper with a district leader as a facilitator/note taker.

4) We provided the attendees with a survey, which they filled out and return to my team.

This information was collected and evaluated by a leadership team who then created a set of recommendations. These recommendations were then vetted by another advisory group consisting of community members, board members, principals, teachers, classified staff, and parents. Once again, their ideas were recorded and amended into the recommendations which would go into the blueprint.

Use of Surveys

We found surveys, either paper, online, or oral, to be a powerful tool for collecting input or feedback. To help you start thinking about the kind of questions you might use with your focus groups, I have included sample survey questions for you in the appendices C3.1. You can use my surveys as a starting place and adapt them for the particular situation in your school or district.

You may want to adapt to reflect your school's administrative hierarchy, the languages represented in your district, how your ESOL program is structured, or the kinds of groups you'd like to survey (It can be especially challenging to create a survey for communities: they all are so different). You can use the questions on my samples surveys as they are, change or add questions, or provide room for teachers to make comments under each category. You might want to create an online survey and allow for your committee to collaborate around the survey findings.

I've already made mention of the survey we created and gave to multiple stakeholders, including administrators, teachers, school staff, students and parents. A blueprint is a living evolving document that continues to grow and change as we try new approaches to problems and seek input. The effort involved in creating this survey was very worthwhile because even though the results were helpful to informing our program development, the process of creating the survey and forming the questions with experts was a great exercise on its own. Going through this process helped us understand what we wanted feedback on, and connected our work to the perceived needs born out of a program review we had done previously.

Tips and Pointers

Whether or not you use surveys, there are a few tips I'd like to offer for conducting your focus groups. First, when conducting focus groups, don't devote too much time giving information about your programs. Build in just enough to inform, but then spend the majority of the meeting listening. People want to feel that their time is valued and they want to give you their opinions. They don't want to be told information and feel that the district isn't serious about receiving feedback. Next, reach out and bring a variety of voices to the table representing all major language groups. 95 percent of your ELs may speak Spanish, but if the other 5 percent speak Russian, they will not appreciate being left out of the process. Another tip is to hold these meetings at times when parents can attend, provide childcare, translation, and consider where the meeting takes place, to ensure parents feel comfortable attending. In my experience, we had Community School Outreach Specialists who have strong relationships with the community, make the phone calls and get parents to attend. That personal touch made all the difference.

Finally, consider writing down the steps you are taking in the blueprint creation process and make it available to staff and parents. I always have the notes scanned and kept in an electronic file where it can be easily accessed. This shows that you are open, fair, and that input is sought and used to help guide decisions.

As you create your focus group activities, think about your parents, community, and EL students. Will you need to translate questions into a language other than English? Are your respondents literate in their native language? Are there cultural biases in your questions, and what biases might you encounter in conducting the focus groups? Some cultures see the teacher as an authority figure not to be challenged: do parents view themselves as partners in their child's education, and will they understand and respond well to the idea of a focus group? What format of questions will be easier for the audience to understand: yes/no, rating on a scale of 1–10, open-ended questions, or some other format? Finding answers to these questions may improve your results and ensure everyone feels valued and able to contribute.

Using Input to Tell a Data Story

With the focus groups you conduct, you will glean a lot of useful information about your program successes and shortcomings. How do district leaders effectively communicate these stories to the right people? From my experience, this is an opportunity for those involved in ELE planning development to become storytellers. That's right – storytellers. Storytellers communicate a need (or a success!), using data to shape and tell their story. Numbers tell simple, raw truths, and the story's impact has greater force when the numbers shape and provide evidence for the tale. Leaders in the role of storyteller paint a picture to their colleagues, communicating the urgency of this work in a way that is both collaborative and positive in spirit. It's like a contractor saying you have a leaky pipe and your floor is damaged—bad news is never good to hear, but when you hear it from the right person, you know you'll have support and help to create a plan to fix the problem. As part of the process of building a blueprint, we create data stories that builds the 'Why' of our work – establishing a sense of urgency and purpose—which is critical to building a collaborative process that unites administrators and educators to help all ELs achieve at high levels.

What is a data story?

We have been talking about data stories but have not formally defined them. So what are they? A data story is a simple but useful tool that aids in telling small stories about the needs or successes of ELs. It is a one-page report with a graphic, usually based on current test data, that helps relay your story in a short, succinct way. It's simple, straight-forward, and serves to back up what you have to say.

You can use a data story to communicate information to a number of groups of people, including your blueprint committee, district administrators, principals, teachers, an advisory committee, etc. A data story can serve as an initial jumping-off point for blueprint creation, a catalyst for conversation with a district or school leader, or means to propose changes to an existing blueprint. Data stories can be used in many situations where conveying a story of need is important in order to move your program forward.

Preparing Your Data Story

In the next few sections, we'll look more closely at the steps in process of creating a data story. Your data story might include relevant data with a source and graphic, a description of issues, talking points, or suggestions for change/improvement. Or, it might provide each school with their EL data and have a short description of the ESOL program, include acronyms, and the basics of serving ELs.

Regardless, to prepare your data story you will need to be aware of who your audience will be. You can create data stories to present to your newly formed blueprint committee; or, you can also create a data story prior to meeting with principals and district leaders to discuss their ELs and ways to assist.

Your data story should have an objective, a reason for telling it. What is your goal? What do you want to communicate? There are two main stories you'll likely be telling.

The *We-Have-Room-For-Improvement Story*: This is often the initial story we bring to our blueprint committees or to our district leaders or school principals: Based on the data, there are a lot of students not doing very well academically, and they need our help – now! We need to act we need to make some changes. The specific data you show needs to instill in your audience (your committee, principals, district leaders) a sense of urgency— the impending crisis involved in not serving and establish a purpose—focusing on the needs of our most vulnerable students.

The *We-Are-Making-Progress Story*: It will be really encouraging to principals and to teachers, who have been working really hard to help ELs, to hear data stories that show growth and progress. This story is one that you'll hopefully get to tell down the road, once you begin to build momentum and see your Blueprint come to life. The specific data you show will demonstrate increased test scores or graduation rates, or decreased absenteeism. The overall message should be one of growth, but keep focusing and working hard to ensure all students reach the standards, etc.

Beware as you analyze data to tell a story, that there are a few pitfalls to be aware of! Rather than creating a story that seems to be true based on experience or anecdotes, carefully assess your data as a whole. Are there alternative explanations for what seems to be a cut-and-dried correlation? Are you making assumptions and using the data to support them? Or are you looking at the data and evaluating them objectively?

Choose Data to Include

These two kinds of stories can have many different variations. Depending on the story you are telling and how you are telling it the data you include in your actual data story may include the following:

- Number of ELs in middle and high school combined and at each school. Of those how many are Long-term ELs, how many are newcomers? How many are dual identified Special Education and ELs? How many are in the Migrant program?
- Number of ELs (not) meeting standards on state assessments in reading, math, and writing
- Number of ELs who have been in ELD for five plus years

- Performance trends for all ELs over a period of years to measure growth
- Performance scores for ELs on state English language proficiency assessments in reading, writing, speaking, and listening
- Number of ELs are attending college (national and district data, if possible)
- The graduation rate for ELs in the district compared to other subgroups (e.g., economically disadvantaged non-ELs, SPED, migrant)

Remember, however, that when you prepare your data story, include just enough data to tell that story—no more, no less. Also remember to cite the sources for your data; this will strengthen the credibility of your message.

Craft your Data Story

Once you've selected a small but relevant set of data to include, it's important to craft the story in a way that will maintain the attention of your audience. Many of the people who will receive your data story are typically data savvy but extremely busy, juggling a lot of information at once. So too many data can quickly become onerous and too much to comprehend. The kindest thing you can do for your busy audience is to create a short, one-page report with clear graphics that addresses the issues at hand in a concise manner.

A good data story is both *visual* and *focused*. By *visual*, I mean that the data should be presented as a graphic that is easy to interpret; it is easily digestible by any of its potential audiences. A data story should also be *focused*—its meanings and conclusions should be narrow and succinct; it should focus on a niche area, rather than attempt to address broad, sweeping issues.

Choose a graphic that best tells your story in an uncomplicated manner, with no unnecessary data, clean lines, and a clear key. A pie chart is an easy way to represent parts of a whole in a given year, e.g., the entire 2015 student body, broken into non-ELs, ELs, and L-TELs. A bar chart can represent the progress of certain groups over a number of years, e.g., graduation rates of L-TELs in one school in the district from 2010 to 2015.

Sometimes it is helpful to your audience if you can put those numbers into terms that will immediately resonate with them. For example, *440 high school students are failing in our district. That amounts to one large elementary school. One whole school in our district is failing. Are we ok with that?* Naturally, you know your audience and how best to conclude your presentation. This may or may not be an effective approach for your group.

You may also want to select a theme to help frame the story you are telling, and you can relay your entire presentation through the lens of this theme. The following are some sample themes and how you might use them:

Theme	Use
Social Science	*The future of our democracy depends on a well-educated and informed electorate.*
Business/Economic	*For our nation to remain competitive in the world, we need to ensure all of our students are successful in school.*
Moral	*We are failing large numbers of children. Are we OK with that?*
Cultural	*We need to embrace these students and make them feel like they are important members of our society who add to our culture. We need to be very aware of the messages we are sending to them if we want them to carry on American traditions and values.*

For each theme, be prepared with some supportive data. For example, if you are presenting from a cultural perspective, you could use the following statements: *The Hispanic population is growing at a large pace* or *The US population will look very different in 20-24 years*. Both of these statements are easily backed up with data from the US Census Bureau. Make sure to provide your sources, in case your audience wants to check your facts.

Keep in mind that a focused, succinct data story with a comprehensible visual graphic can lead to a productive conversation regarding the school's (or district's) ELs.

Presenting Your Data Story

Because each school is different and has a different EL population, my conversations around the data story often vary. I give a general description of what their population looks like, which leads to differing conversations about support. One high school with a high population of English Learners, for example, might need to consider adding an algebra support class if the data is showing that large numbers of their ELs are failing, while another school with 4 ELs we might be talking about strategically training a core group of content teachers who will receive these ELs in their classrooms and ensure that sheltered strategies are provided throughout the day for these students. Generally, however, my message includes the following points and questions:

- Our long-term ELs are a diverse group requiring different supports; who needs what, for how long?
- Too many ELs are struggling; how can we best support them throughout their day/schooling?
- Data story about one or two sub-groups (e.g., dual-identified SPED and EL students, or long-term ELs); how the district can support; what the school is doing and needs?

Once you have presented the message, the discussion is open for topics related to the ELE blueprint. Some possible discussion topics include the following examples:

1. Instructors: We need to ensure that our ELD staff are focused on supporting their students with the language necessary for success. Instructors should have ample planning time and the time and support necessary to be and feel successful. This supports quality instruction.

2. Equity: We need to ensure that we are supporting all of our ELs to be successful and feel valued as contributing members of our schools. This speaks to building a culture of equity and inclusiveness that permeates the school.

3. Supports and Interventions: We look at our dual identified ELs and understand how to best provide services to these potentially overlooked groups. This illustrates a focus on the individual child.

4. Data Use: Likewise, for certain groups of ELs, such as those in the Migrant Program, we want to examine the data to learn more about them: how many days each year they have been attending; how long they have been in our district; whether or not they are considered Priority One as described above, and so on.

These are all examples of topics I might discuss in our meeting. We may only focus on one of these topics during the initial meeting, but consider what foundation has been laid here for ongoing conversations with one simple Data Story:

-   We have highlighted a group that badly needs additional support.
-   We have called attention to students who are dual identified and have begun discussing solutions.
-   We can discuss instruction, go on "learning walks," where teachers or administrators observe other classrooms, and continue what supports for PD are needed and make a plan.

In short, whatever discussion we have is productive and assisting English Learners succeed. We are drilling down further to understand the root causes of what is keeping them from progressing linguistically, and we are coming up with possible solutions.

The combination of a short data story and a productive, informative conversation will likely leave your audience feeling that their time has been well spent. Also, they will respect you as a source of relevant and concise information.

A Data Story Example from Salem-Keizer

At Salem-Keizer, one of the groups we wanted to learn more about and assist was long-term ELs (students who had failed to exit ELD after having been in the class for 5 or more years). The following example provides some insight into the data story I developed and presented for the Salem-Keizer schools.

When I first came to Salem-Keizer, our high schools staff and administration were not being as focused and intentional with our English Learners as they could be, and it showed in their data. ELs were not being challenged and engaged and many were not on track to graduate. Federal Title III law says ELs should be exiting an ELD program around the five-year mark – at least that's the goal we are held to—and Salem Keizer was failing on those stats. Through research, I knew that language acquisition can take more like 5-7 years, and even longer for students who have special needs, or significant gaps in education. I knew the SK situation needed to improve, but how exactly?

Process

To examine how Salem-Keizer's students were faring in light of these pieces of policy and research, I decided to gather data on how our ELs were doing in state summative reading and math assessments and graduation rates data compared to their white and Asian peers. I had a data committee and we worked with our Testing and Evaluation Department, pulling records from our district database, and then analyzing the data for performance trends.

I then looked at how long it was taking our ELs to reach proficiency, and then I focused in on the high school students. Most of our ELs were being promoted out of ELD prior to reaching high school, but the ones who remained, who were they? What was their story and what supports did they need to exit?

In reviewing these data, I made a decision to focus a beginning conversation on high school long-term ELs - students who had been in the district since elementary school. They represented the majority of ELs in the high schools, and I wanted us, as a team, to focus on who these students are and what supports they needed to successfully exit ELD.

I had my team create infographics - one for each high school, that quickly and visually told a story, so that when I visited with the principal, we could start talking about the issues and solutions for serving these students. An example of one of those graphics is listed below.

Presentation

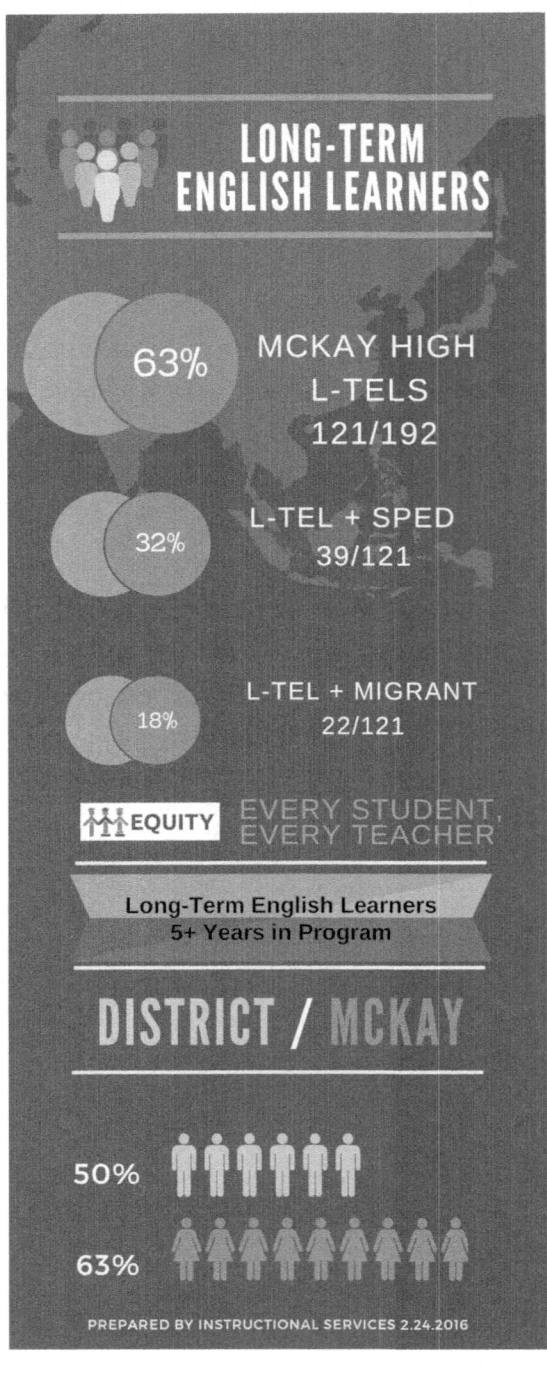

While I wanted my conversation with the district principals to build awareness around long-term ELs, I also wanted to go a little deeper and discuss the needs of the LTEL subgroups. So I broke the LTEL cohort into subgroups, and begin discussing potential solutions and ways the district is able to support each kind of LTEL, whether they are on an Individualized Education Plan (IEP), or migrant, or just a product of not receiving the right supports along-the-way.

I didn't bring a magic solution to solve these problems, but I believe that when we focus on these students as individuals and become intentional is supports and interventions, we can make a difference.

Outcomes

As a result of the data story and conversation with the principals, we formed a Long-term EL Workgroup that focused on solutions at our high schools. Members included administrative representation from each high school and the English Language Acquisition Specialists that served each school. Reflecting the Core Value of being Focused and Intentional, we determined which ELs who were dual identified, where they were located, and what their designation was (LRC, EGC, etc.). In conjunction with the Special Education Department, the workgroup performed classroom observations, talked with SPED Case Managers about their students, and enquired about professional development needs. We discussed options for severely disabled students in self-contained classrooms who are unable to take yearly summative assessments. Finally, the workgroup helped teachers of ELD classrooms to plan and differentiate instruction so they feel more successful.

I decided to combine the migrant specialists, who are charged with supporting migrant students in those schools with the largest Migrant populations, with the English Language Acquisition Specialists (ELAS), who serve as instructional coaches in every high school. Both groups met and we made a plan to coordinate efforts. As a result, all of our long-term EL/Migrant students were able to meet with both staff persons together. They discussed their graduation path and their annual language assessment (ELPA 21), and offered encouragement to succeed.

To address those LTELS what were not dual-identified, the workgroup used the data to inform the ELD teachers of how long these students had been in ELD and to suggest where they needed to focus. Each school piloted a 'Continuity of Care' effort (which will be discussed at length in Chapter 8) to have more adults reach out to these students in an effort to offer encouragement and support.

To keep principals informed of these efforts and changes, I provided them with a one-page summary (short, succinct, and focused!) detailing what we were planning during the year, along with a goal of meeting our long-term EL target.

ACTIVITY 1: Seeking Input

This first activity involves setting up your first community advisory group meeting or series of meetings. Have your Leadership Committee meet and discuss the following questions (again, you may have other questions you want to ask - these questions are intended to help structure the conversation).

- How many meetings will be held over what time span?
- What are the objectives for this first meeting?
- What information will be shared and what questions will be asked?
- What format will you use to convey information and seek feedback? (World Cafe?)
- Who will organize and who will facilitate the meetings?
- Who will interpret?
- Who will do childcare?
- How will this information be recorded and reported out?

ACTIVITY 2: Creating a Data Story

Objective: Prepare a Data Story that will compliment a presentation to your focus groups

Desired Outcome: To build awareness, generate dialogue, and instill a sense of urgency.

Possible Key Points for Presentation:

1. The Hispanic population is growing exponentially. (Discuss what the population of the U.S. will look like in 20–40 years.

2. Possible themes:

a. Social Science: Discuss the future of our Democracy and needing a well-educated and informed electorate.

b. Business/Economic: To remain competitive in the world, we need to ensure all of our students are successful in school.

c. Moral: We are failing large numbers of children. Are we OK with that?

d. Cultural: We need to embrace these students and make them feel like they are important members of our society; that they add to our culture. We need to be very aware of the messages we are sending to them if we want them to carry on American traditions and values.

3. Data: Show how many ELs are attending college (national and district data, if possible)

4. Data: Show graduation rate for ELs in the district compared to other subgroups

5. Data: Show the total number of ELs in the district and show how many of them are underachieving.

6. Put the total number into terms that will resonate with your audience. Example: 440 high school students are failing in our district. That amounts to one large elementary school. One whole school in our district is failing. Are we Okay with that? (Naturally, you know your audience and how best to conclude your presentation. This approach may not be the right approach for you, but you get the idea.

Reminders: Whether you provide a handout or project a slide, you want a colorful, concise, 'snapshot' of data that illustrates what you are saying; nothing more.

CHAPTER 4

Leadership and Professional Development

Chapter Objectives:

- To identify and discuss key leadership elements necessary for ensuring schools have the focus and intentionality needed to be successful in educating ELs.
- To evaluate your current professional development model at both the district and school level to see how it aligns with the needs of your ELs.

Research is clear and abundant on how impactful quality leadership can be on a school's success, and we read the testimony from school administrators reinforcing this idea in chapter one. I would argue that the importance of leadership in supporting structures that ensure ELs are successful is also profound, especially in being focused and intentional relative to the vision, supporting staff, and continually promoting equity. This chapter focuses on a few specific areas where leadership can make a difference in building quality ESOL programs, and it discusses the importance of quality professional development and what to consider at the district level (view from the mountain top) as well as the school level (view from ground level).

The Importance of Quality Leadership

As Rosalynn Carter said, "A leader takes people where they want to go. A great leader takes people where they don't necessarily want to go, but ought to be." Anyone can create a great plan, program, or school, but without effective leadership, nothing is going to improve or be truly impactful. Changing conditions for English Learners and ensuring the environment is rich for academic and personal achievement is hard work, and as leaders, you need a strong collaborative voice – one that sets the tone for high achievement and for equity.

Because I believe the ultimate success of any ELE program stems from the support it receives from all levels, the definition of leadership I'm using for this chapter is broad. I'm defining a leader as anyone in district leadership, from the district superintendent, to the principal of the high school. Top district leadership holds the key to ensuring that ELs are a priority, that initiatives are set in motion, and that a strong collaborative tone is set.

Create Focus and intentionality

After reading the Core Value section related to being Focused, Intentional and Results Oriented in chapter one, we know how successful schools can be when this concept is applied.

If you have one takeaway from this book, I hope it is the idea that being successful equates to being focused and intentional in your efforts to set ELs up for success. From a district perspective, focused means that district leadership is working together with this singular goal in mind. I'm not suggesting that it is the only goal just that it's on the tongue of all conversations related to student achievement. EL achievement cannot reside in one office with a small team trying to support ELs. Likewise, in schools, EL success cannot reside with the ELD teacher alone. To be focused means that whenever we discuss improvements in instruction we are not segmenting ELs as an add-on group that also needs some attention. We shouldn't approach ELs as a certain group that needs additional support from a few people who have specialized training in sheltered strategies. To do so will equate to a continuation of mediocre achievement.

Intentional means that we have articulated plans that address the needs of ELs and that everyone in the district and in the schools is aware of these plans and are working as one body toward these goals.

When it comes to solving the EL issue, it's important to know that there is not one way of being successful. To that end, it doesn't matter what researched based path you take to solve the achievement gap, as long as you stay true to that path and implement it with fidelity.

Salem-Keizer's leadership has been focusing on several key areas over the last few years: communicating the ideas in the blueprint, working on professional development, using data, and promoting educational equity. In this chapter, we'll examine how the focus and intentionality of leadership affect those goals.

Develop and Communicate the vision

The primary responsibility of leadership is to develop, understand, and communicate the vision for ELs in the district or school. As mentioned earlier, the blueprint team or leader creates a visual presentation of the blueprint and then meets with all EL stakeholders who directly work with ELs, such as ELD teachers, counselors and registrars for scheduling purposes, and so on.

In addition, the blueprint and vision for the ESOL program may change as you seek ongoing evaluation and improvement. When there is need for change, the committee or leader will be responsible for revising the blueprint vision documents and relaying those changes. The committee or leader may also create and revise guiding documents and rubrics for administrators to provide them a "measuring stick" to determine progress.

Leadership at the school level also acts in the role of facilitator and cheer-leader, emulating commitment to the plan by keeping all relevant staff focused on the vision and supporting them in being successful. For example, when developing an instructional focus with your staff, give them time to plan, review data and reflect, and then protect them from activities, meetings, and new initiatives that can distract them from their work.

Another example would be coming up with shared belief statements, like, "As a learning community, we believe in engaging and supporting all students to be successful," and incorporating those belief statements in all team planning times.

One final example would be having the leader introduce short video clips or TED Talks, or short articles on equity or teaching diverse learners at each staff meeting. Perhaps an equity discussion question could also be discussed at each staff meeting. From that work, some teachers might want to do a book study, or prepare a short presentation for a future staff meeting. Whatever method you choose, the point is that equity is on the minds of the staff throughout the year and not just introduced and then forgotten.

Use K–12 Articulation

The Focused and Intentional & Results Oriented Core Value discussed in chapter 1 includes the idea of Shared Responsibility and Collaboration as being a crucial part of a good ELE plan—bringing together a team of leaders from across the district to ensure EL success. This idea of planning, vision, and collaboration across all levels— elementary to middle to high school—is known as K–12 articulation. Each level may have different priorities, but the goal is for all levels to work together.

The Connecticut State Board of Education issued position statement on developing a collaborative approach to leadership, which states, "District leaders must establish and support effective leadership structures that include all members of the school district team. The new leadership paradigm must move districts and schools toward becoming a collaborative learning community, focused on student learning. (Marzano, Waters 2009, p.72). Marzano and Waters (2009) go on to write, "Without the involvement of these groups in an atmosphere of creative problem solving regarding the singular goal of enhancing student achievement, little of substance can be accomplished." (p.72)

Collaborative goal setting means that all leaders across all grades are hearing the same messages and asked to deliver and enforce those messages in their buildings, using a similar approach. The messages received by teachers in the district reflect solidarity in purpose – a district vision that emulates equity and success for all children. It is a vision that shows teachers that the district is serious about ensuring all students succeed and that there is a plan to support them to be successful in that regard.

Promote educational equity

As leaders, we need to lead by example and be clear and intentional about learning and what is possible when we come together to challenge and support our students who are adding a second language. To that end, I recommend that leaders focus on the Core Value of Educational Equity, as described in chapter one —that all students need to be given the opportunity for an equal education— and building this idea into all training.

Many of you support teachers who understand the challenges English Learners face, but not everyone understands second language acquisition or how best to support ELs – especially when the issues are compounded by the effects of poverty, violence, gang activity, etc. Humans often make judgments based on limited experiences, which can lead to incorrect assumptions -- even among well-meaning and intentioned professionals.

Good leaders understand ELs issues and incorrect assumptions they face: this is key to providing educational equity. As with instruction, the challenge is to promote educational equity in a way that is not burdensome to your teachers and staff. Time investment, follow through, or money involved often surface as barriers.

But focusing on equity in the classroom is readily achievable and it can serve as a gateway to being culturally competent (e.g. acceptance and respect for differences; continual assessment of sensitivity to other cultures; expansion of knowledge; hiring a diverse and unbiased staff). I should add that not only is a focus on equity achievable, it's imperative if we are to ensure the success of our ELs.

Beginning the Equity Conversation

One approach to building awareness around equity involves having a staff read articles or a book together to spark discussion and promote understanding. While this approach is good, it's important to consider the readings a place to begin the conversation, and not be the conversation. In other words, it's not enough to read and discuss - action really must follow. For example, after reading a book or article, follow up by having the staff craft a shared definition and action items that everyone commits to doing, such as incorporating the definition of equity into every PD workshop district coaches provide, or having a set of guiding principles staff use regularly throughout the year. One example of a book you may want to examine is Scheurich, J.J., & Skrla, L. (2003). *Leadership for equity and excellence: Creating high-achievement in classrooms, schools, and districts.* Thousand Oaks, CA: Corwin Press and Linton, C. (2011). Equity 101. Thousand Oaks, CA: Corwin Press.

After your group reads a book on equity, the planning that follows can lead to agreements on what supports are needed for ELs that foster a dynamic and ongoing discourse on equity in the classroom. Conversations might include a different approach to planning lessons that includes nonfiction articles written from different cultural perspectives; or establishing background knowledge by bringing in or eliciting examples from the cultures represented in your classroom.

When we have a common understanding of equity and begin discussing what is -- or is not in place instructionally for ELs to ensure they meet and exceed the standards – that is the beginning of awareness which can lead to the evolution of practice.

Building a family

When I think of equity, the example of a family comes to mind. I am fortunate to be a father of three beautiful children. While considering equity in our schools, I sometimes compare it to a family with three children and ask what it would be like if two children were praised, given all the emotional and organizational and linguistic support needed; given attention - encouraged to go to college, etc., while denying the third child the same attention and opportunities. Of course, we would never act that way towards our own children. But in truth, our ELs are our children. They are part of our school family. Why then are we not giving them all of the support and encouragement we give to other students? I realize in some places we are - but in others, there is a difference. Many ELs are still underrepresented in AP and IB classes. Many are not given the language supports or the structured writing supports they need to be successful in their content classes. Too many suffer from poor self-esteem and think they are stupid, or that college is unreachable. The achievement and opportunity gaps still exist throughout this country, which tells me that some children are still not truly accepted as an important family member.

I think it's also worth noting that in addition to language challenges and having their culture valued and included in instruction, ELs are also trying to be accepted by their peers and often dealing with life issues and the effects of poverty that make day-to-day survival very difficult.

As leaders, one of the ways to provide equity is to intentionally treat ELs like a member of your family. No one on your staff would let one of their own children fail or suffer in some way, and the same should be true for all of your students. Taking a family approach, where all students are engaged in active learning, held to the same expectations of achievement, and supported both academically and emotionally, will go a long way to helping ELs feel welcomed, accepted, and honored.

Tap Teachers with an Equity Mindset

Be intentional about identifying and communicating with certain teachers who have an equity approach to planning and teaching all students. Ask them what kind of support they would need in terms of collaboration, planning time, professional development, etc., and begin to build a cohort of teachers in every grade level, and in every subject area who will be your core block and then move to expand from there. Being intentional about creating a strong cohort of passionate teachers who enjoy teaching in a way that allows all students to learn and thrive, takes time and effort in some cases, but it's important work that will pay dividends.

Ensure proper placement of ELs

Be very intentional about student placement in core subject classes. In schools with low to medium numbers of ELs, look to cluster them in groups of five to eight in with your cohort of identified teachers. If every class in your school has large numbers of ELs, then clustering may not be appropriate, unless you look at more at-risk students and carefully place them in with teachers who are inspirational and supportive. This does take effort, but shared between an administrator and perhaps an EL lead teacher and a counselor or registrar, it is very doable.

Involve Community

Remember to reach out to your community. Bringing in parents of migrant students or other ELs may be a constant challenge for a variety of reasons, but know that they are concerned about their child's education and they really enjoy when they are listened to and when their opinions are sought. I have worked with migrant families for many years, I've traveled around Oregon talking with parents in different districts, and my takeaway has been that many school districts try to reach them and talk at them about Title IA etc., but few spend the time listening and asking for their opinions and advice. Just know that a little effort can yield great results, even if those results are only felt among the three families that attend your meeting. Also, don't be discouraged by low turnout, but continue to build relationships and see this work as a process that takes time. Take the time to get to know the cultures you are working with and go out to where they are gathering. Remember the example from chapter one when Principal Olga Cobb went to the Russian church to make connections with that community. Her efforts resulted in building strong Russian parent involvement in her school.

Set high expectations for ELs

While ELs may struggle with the English language, they have the same capabilities as any other group of students, and they need to be treated as such. I have seen high school students with low self-esteem, clumped together in sheltered classrooms and all placed in the same hallway, where the instruction was less than rigorous and followed a different set of standards. I also encountered high school teachers who conveyed to me that 'these kids' couldn't make it in a regular class, while others who agreed. felt they needed to be protected and not 'thrown to the wolves.'

Conversely, in the same district, I observed most ELs performing very well across all 11 middle schools where sheltered classrooms had been abolished for intermediate levels 3 and 4 for several years, and where sheltered strategies were promoted, supported, enforced, and evaluated throughout the school. In talking with some of these teachers, they all spoke about the importance of having the same expectations for all their students. It was clear that ELs were just part of the family. They were included, accepted, and challenged like everyone else, and their summative data told the story. It's a classic example of when we hold all of our kids to the same high expectations and provide the proper supports and scaffolds, ELs will benefit in multiple ways.

Set Non-negotiable Priorities for Accountability

Wherever we focus our energies, we are going to see improvement. It's important that every principal set a tone of high expectations, of academic rigor, engagement, and support for all students in the school. To that end, certain practices need to be in place so that ELs can feel valued and so they can access the content.

What I'm offering here, is that building cultural awareness and equity is about an intentional shift in thinking that infuses equity throughout everything one does in district and school professional development.

How powerful could it be to have all department chairs in a leadership team comprise a list of what is non-negotiable in every classroom and then have the staff provide input and come to a common agreement? Consider the following examples:

- All students will graduate from high school and be college and career ready.
- Students will be active learners and routinely engage in academic conversations that lead to writing.

- All students will have the individual support they need to reach and exceed the standards.
- All Students will be held accountable for their learning in every class.

It's difficult to argue with the goals listed above. Even so, you may have broad acceptance to the ideas but disagreement by some when it comes to understanding what it takes to ensure these goals become a reality. Don't worry about getting everyone right away. Begin by having staff agree to a set of shared beliefs and focus on this list throughout the year. As you look to bring on new staff, you are looking through this lens and crafting your questions accordingly.

In Salem-Keizer, for example, all of my coaches use a document they created called, The Guiding Principles of Equity, when they plan their workshops. Having teachers and coaches be purposeful in building equity, means that one is always using the definition and its characteristics into trainings, unit and lesson planning, and professional discussions, on a consistent basis.

In summary, figure out as a leadership team what your priorities are, and then hold teachers accountable through stated expectations, through observations and evaluations. It has been my observation that teachers improve in areas where they are held consistently accountable, and where they receive the needed support to be successful.

Supporting Professional Development from the Mountain Top

Teachers and administrators are busy people and they have perhaps one of the most demanding jobs in our society. It's important that a well-implemented program include well-planned professional development (PD) that values their time and respects the challenges of their jobs. The district needs to develop a focused, specific plan for professional development and clearly communicate that to teachers, who can trust it will stay in place over a sustained period of time (with natural adjustments as needed). The training needs to be relevant, focused, and considered a valuable use of time. Teachers require more than a single exposure to new ideas and strategies, so a plan for professional development should extend throughout the year.

In Salem-Keizer, we provided a series of trainings over a semester. Teachers had time to practice (we required it as an assignment) and bring their questions to the next session. Coaches were available during the week to answer questions, model lessons, and observe and give feedback. Following the trainings, each cohort was provided a series of "Touchback" sessions throughout the year. The group would decide in which areas to explore in more depth, and work as a PLC with the coach.

In addition to understanding the big picture, leaders also partner with schools regarding their professional development needs. In this capacity, leadership exercises focus and intentionality by helping to set goals regarding EL students, determine what resources would help teachers better serve ELs, assess how well teachers understand the challenges their students face, and find out if the school's instructional coaches are being well utilized.

Planning

One of the responsibilities of leadership is to ensure that the planning phase intentionally addresses a number of details that are critical to program success. Among those are including the ESOL department, creating an appropriately narrow focus, appropriate budgeting, and wise use of personnel. In my experience, these are the main issues that should be addressed to adequately support professional development.

Include the ESOL department

If EL numbers are low, we may be tempted to downplay the need for professional development around EL instruction. After all, aren't there other groups of students who need support, students whose primary language is English and who need to be pushed so they are prepared for college? Focusing on just ELs means that we could be excluding the others, right? For example, if a school has 10 ELs, does that school really need to have the same emphasis on specific instructional strategies and scaffolding that the Title IA school with 500 ELs down the road need?

There are two ways to look at this question. First, because there are many ways to address the myriad challenges associated with ELs, it's essential to meaningfully include the ESOL department as an equal partner in professional development discussions, regardless of the size of your EL population. This strategy will ensure that your ELs are given a chance at success and inclusion in district efforts.

Second, professional development sessions that promote quality, effective instruction are needed for ALL students, not just ELs. If leadership asks teachers to use data to make informed decisions, plan units and lessons to build supports for all learners, engaging students and igniting their passion for learning; holding all students accountable to the learning; helping students write, comprehend, and communicate orally; checking for understanding and re-teaching when necessary - these steps will benefit not only ELs, but also the larger student population.

Effective instruction is good for all learners, but it is essential for English Learners. Rather than suggest that a school does not need professional development on effective instruction because it has only a handful of ELs, we should consider the benefits to the larger student population. We may not need to provide as many language scaffolds in that scenario, but the approach can still be fairly similar across the district.

For example, a school with a small population of ELs may decide to focus on writing without realizing that ELs actually need an approach that is more structured and explicit—at least initially. While many English teachers shudder at the idea of teaching a program that is too formulaic, what they don't understand is that many students, especially ELs, need to learn the formula, the structure, for good writing before they can express themselves more completely. Additionally, most cultures around the world approach essay writing very differently than we here in the U.S. To not explicitly explain how to construct a paragraph and stretch that into an essay is somewhat like giving a beginning cook the ingredients without providing the recipe.

Narrow Your Focus

There are many possible avenues of professional development, and teachers can only take on so much at one time, given their student load, required prep time, and other obligations. Asking teachers to focus on multiple initiatives concurrently like, Sheltered Instruction Observational Protocol (SIOP), or Positive Behavior Interventions and Supports (PBIS), or other literacy or cultural competency strategies, etc., can lead a staff to feel overwhelmed, shut down, and want to return to their known and comfortable ways of teaching. They may add a strategy here and an understanding there but may not incorporate practical changes as quickly as ELs will need it. Leadership should work to create a professional development scope that is as narrow as possible, working on small pieces at a time, or combining several ideas into one easy-to-implement PD strategy.

In the ESOL Department at Salem-Keizer, we purposefully combined the language of competing district initiatives into our training to help teachers and administrators see the connections and show that we are not introducing several competing initiatives, but similar and common areas of focus with different names. In this particular training, we developed a Concept Sort that had small groups of participants do the work of aligning the different initiatives.

The chart below provides an example of what our teachers might construct from this activity, showing where the similar language or goals intersect.

For example, our district invests a great deal of time and resources on a program called Advancement Via Individual Determination (AVID). While AVID is a program used within a school, common strategies can be incorporated across the school, called WICOR, which stands for Writing, Inquiry, Collaboration, Organization, and Reading. While our district is implementing WICOR strategies, teachers are also taking time to learn a series of literacy strategies, and for those taking our sheltered instruction trainings, receive vocabulary and concepts described in the SIOP approach.

AVID's WICOR Features (Writing, Inquiry, Collaboration, Organization, Reading)	Salem-Keizer's Literacy Model	Sheltered Instruction Observation Protocol (SIOP)
Teacher Directed Instruction	Teacher Directed Instruction Purposeful instruction is a practice in which the teacher deliberately explains and demonstrates the invisible processes, knowledge and skills used in effective reading and writing.	Teacher Directed Instruction Use a variety of techniques to make content concepts clear - modeling, hands-on materials, visuals, film clips, etc.

Writing	Writing	Writing
Students who write demonstrate understanding	Purposeful instruction is a practice in which the teacher deliberately explains and demonstrates the invisible processes, knowledge and skills used in effective reading and writing.	
Questioning	Questioning	Questioning
Inquiry is asking critical questions	Critical thinking is making judgments that are thoughtful and well-founded. It is more than opinion; critical thinking is evaluating text and constructing meaning from it.	Employ a variety of question types - use Question Cube, Thinking Cube, Bloom's Taxonomy etc.
Sharing of Ideas	Sharing of Ideas	Sharing of Ideas
Collaboration is sharing of ideas, information, and opinions		Provide frequent opportunities for interaction and discussion

Assessment and Self-Assessment Students who organize use self-direction and self-evaluation	Assessment and Self-Assessment	Assessment and Self-Assessment Conduct assessment of student comprehension and learning - student self-assessment, quick reviews: thumbs up-down; numbered wheels; small dry erase boards, etc.
Reading Reading is gaining meaning, understanding, and knowledge from print and other media.	Reading Authentic reading is reading a variety of text for real purposes. Authentic reading is most like that which occurs in everyday life	Reading Adapt content to all levels of student proficiency - use graphic organizers, study guides, jigsaw reading, etc.
Purposeful Speaking	Purposeful Speaking Purposeful speaking and listening is the foundation of reading and writing development in which students formally and informally, comprehend, express, and exchange ideas for a variety of authentic purposes.	Purposeful Speaking Provide activities for students to apply content/language knowledge - students listen and discuss in pairs or small groups, making abstract concepts concrete.

In pointing out the similarities, we focused on key instructional strategies that we believed held the greatest impact in the classroom. Helping teachers see how to focus their learning so that it made sense and so it didn't seem like several disconnected approaches were being thrown at them, was appreciated as evidenced from our exit surveys.

The key here, I've learned, is to be very focused on one or two initiatives as a staff and to consistently follow-through with these focal areas, and build each year.

Implementation

The implementation phase is important to the success of your professional development plans. Good leaders provide teachers and staff with small successes and supports during the implementation phase to ensure that they see results and feel successful in the new endeavor.

Implementing PD is challenging because it takes time, buy-in, energy, focus, and holding staff accountable, and just when progress is being made, teaches leave and new ones come on board. That said, however, if the learning becomes part of the school's culture - it's just how business is done at the school and when interviewing prospective new teachers, you can talk about your culture and focus, and gauge how knowledgeable or willing they are to be part of your culture. Additionally, if your staff embraces the vision of a focused, long-term plan and can see the benefits in student learning, then you're on a solid path. Implementation of PD needs to be done in phases and teachers need support along the way, as I describe in the next section.

Ensure ongoing learning

Regardless of what system you put into place, you need to intentionally support teachers in continue the learning process and that they are open to continuous evaluation and improvement. Sometimes a single session on a technique will not be enough; you will have to follow up on implementation.

As an example, when I first came into my job at Salem-Keizer, we had a system whereby teachers were trained in SIOP over a three-day period. In our classroom walkthroughs of teachers who received the training, we often saw little evidence of SIOP. After further thought, we realized the issue: there was no follow up to the training. We concluded that teachers need more than a one-time training!

Over time, we changed our SIOP professional development to last over eight sessions throughout a semester. After each session, teachers would be asked to try certain strategies and then bring back their questions and experiences to share with the group at the next session. Additionally, I placed a specialized instructional coach, called an English Language Acquisition Specialist (ELAS) at each high school. This person would be responsible for delivering the PD and then she/he would continue with that cohort of teachers even after the sessions were complete. In essence, that group of teachers was given a full year of professional development and support.

I believe SIOP and similar methods have value and my staff continues to provide professional development incorporating these strategies. It is my experience and belief, however, that it is not the strategies themselves that lack merit, but the manner in which they are implemented, prioritized, and supported that counts.

Stay the course

While planning for a narrowly focused professional development is important, during the implementation phase, it's important to stick to those few ideas over a period of several years. The Core Value of commitment of the plan over time is important—because we want our teachers to get used to new techniques and see them bear fruit, rather than jumping into a new trend every few months.

In some of the districts where I've worked, the teachers felt that the district was always requiring them to do something new or different. This would have been okay in their minds if leadership stayed focused on those initiatives and saw them through until they could be well implemented. Unfortunately, in the teachers' experience, every year or two district leadership would abandon those great ideas for new ideas. They became jaded and decided to do what they felt was best.

Having been asked to be a lead teacher of a Small Learning Community (SLC), I spent a lot of time going to these veteran teachers and trying to convince them to embrace learning targets and other initiatives the district was promoting. I received polite smiles.

Unfortunately, in this instance, they were correct. After two years, Small Learning Communities disappeared and so did many of the ideas like Learning Targets. This is what we have to avoid. We do not need to create a group of skeptics who choose to 'wait it out.'

Teachers must see that we are in a new era of teaching – that we are dedicated to making pedagogically sound, researched-based changes over the long haul (in line with the Castañeda standard) in order to engage our learners and ignite their love and passion of learning.

Provide coaching support

Having led a team of coaches, what we at Salem-Keizer call English Language Acquisition Specialists, for the past eight years, I can say that using the coaching model is critical, but difficult to do effectively. What follows are some of the key factors to consider when using this model:

Choosing the Right People

The role of ELAS is a critical role that requires special and unique skills that most people don't possess out-of-the-gate. Knowing that each person hired brings certain skills and experience – but not all the skills necessary – means that you have to build and support your coaches as they are placed in the schools. When I hire a coach, they have to have some foundational experience in having worked with ELs, yes, but above all, they must be outgoing and personable. Teachers have to feel really comfortable with these folks because they are being extremely vulnerable and trusting. If this person cannot relate well to the teachers and help them to move their practice, then a key component of your vision for improvement comes to a complete halt. While I'm interviewing coaching candidates I'm frequently envisioning myself as a teacher meeting this person and really trying to see how they come across. Would I feel safe with this person? Would I seek them out for help? Can I trust this person to keep our work and discussions confidential from administrators and my peers? While it's not always possible to discern these qualities in an interview, it is a lens I use.

As an aside, I have found that coaches who come from elementary schools are often not well received in the high schools initially, due to the lack of 'street cred' with respect to secondary instruction, and secondary students and their needs. Also, elementary coaches, although perhaps outstanding and eager for the challenge, sometimes come in having to earn that respect - and that can take time. I have introduced middle school coaches and teachers as high school coaches, and it usually takes several months to be accepted, but they eventually do. Elementary coaches sometimes never do make the shift - it depends a lot on the individual. I'm sure it's probably the same for high school coaches going to the elementary level as well. I'm not sure why, exactly, but it is a reality that merits discussion ahead-of-time.

Defining the Role

These coaches are placed in a situation where the need is extremely great. On any given day, they could be asked to get involved in so many tasks that they cease in being effective. If a coach is going to help to close the achievement gap for ELs in a high school, their role must be focused, specific, and manageable. If this is not the case, then it's a waste of valuable resources. They must also never be perceived as pseudo-administrators - not if you are serious about helping students improve.

My ELAS are asked to coach no more than 5-8 individuals at any given time, and they receive ongoing professional development on transformational coaching – how to really take teachers of all levels and ability to the next level of professional growth.

They are asked to create and provide professional development. This is very time consuming and can take them away from getting into classrooms. The key here is to have specific time allotted where they can develop trainings, and keep the rest of the week sacred for getting into classrooms. It's important not to give all of the PD responsibility for the school to the coach. It's better for the coach to work with teachers on planning for PD, rather than being the person solely responsible. Additionally, the PD provided should connect with the work outlined by the ESL team. If a principal or leader wants this person to give unrelated PD either to his staff or staff in a district training, this only stretches the coach further and can completely stress them out to the point that they feel unsuccessful.

Communicating the Role

If coaches specializing in helping ELs are to remain happy in their jobs and feel successful, and if in fact they are to make a tangible difference, they cannot serve two masters with different visions. It is absolutely imperative that coaches are supervised and directed by the ESL Coordinator; the Coordinator, however, must communicate often and well with the principals to ensure everyone is working toward the same goal. Communicating the ESOL Blueprint so that everyone knows the work and understands how to focus the resources is difficult, time consuming, but essential to success.

Staying on Course

I alluded to the fact that coaches can be spread very thin very quickly making them ineffective. Coaches themselves feel very responsible for helping kids and often take on jobs that aren't listed in the job description. For example, coaches sometimes want to help the testing coordinator and make sure everyone is scheduled for their summative testing; if they miss the test, they want to call home and re-schedule. Perhaps they get involved in placing new students, and making sure all active ELs are in ELD class. Does a parent want to disclaim services? These coaches will want to have those conversations with parents and students. Are students failing? They will want to be the ones who have conversations with the students and with the teachers. Many issues arise each day that can easily involve them. The point we must remember is that the more they do that does not involve classroom coaching, the less impact they are having in helping to change classroom practices. It's not that those pieces aren't important that I mentioned, but the coach's time is limited and focused. The more diluted it becomes, the worse the situation gets. Additionally, when school administrators tell their coach to help the math department, or go in a different direction that keeps this limited resource occupied in a way that is not focused on ELs specifically, the person becomes less impactful.

Make use of PLCs

Another way to enhance and support instruction is to make use of professional learning communities (PLCs), which you may already have in your schools. Ken Parshall refers to these collaborative teacher groups in relation to McKay High School as described earlier in this chapter. At Salem-Keizer, we found that bringing all ELD teachers together in a district-wide PLC several times throughout the year was time well spent, and increased our impact on student learning. This environment of shared responsibility and collaboration allowed us to:

- Plan units together with instructional coaches and/or English Language Acquisition Specialists (ELAS) using a template created with ELs in mind
- Bring singleton ELD teachers together with colleagues from around the district to feel part of a learning community.
- Bring new ELD teachers together to receive quality planning and instructional knowledge.
- Bring our veteran teachers together to continue to their ongoing development.

Additionally, these district PLCs afforded us the opportunity to convey the big picture of our Blueprint and helped our teachers see how they fit into the larger picture of EL achievement. Teachers worked side-by-side with their instructional coach and with their ELD colleagues to build engaging units that contain of all the necessary elements to be effective. We found through surveys after each meeting that our teachers really value this time together and we also noticed that they were always extremely focused and on-task.

Establish teacher accountability

In hard economic times, it's sometimes difficult to provide ample time for teachers to learn and improve on their craft. Teaching, and doing it effectively, is no doubt one of the hardest and most complex jobs around – but then I'm speaking to the choir. Having said that, teaching in a traditional sense – lecture, and expecting students to read texts, take notes, and do well on quizzes and tests, was never really effective practice for most students, but it's been our model of choice for the last 100 years.

As a parent, and having observed numerous high school classrooms, I continue to see a majority of teachers talking most of the time and students passively taking in information. I see multiple chapters in textbooks assigned without help on how to read a text, or guides on what concepts will be on the test. I see information in lecture given without a solid note taking strategy in place. Even in classrooms where Cornell Notes are being incorporated, they frequently don't revisit the notes the next day or later in the week. I've seen history PowerPoint lectures that cover a lot of ground and include hard vocabulary and concepts like propaganda covered in one class period, where students were asked to take a quiz at the end to see if they were listening. I see classrooms where high academic vocabulary and language functions like, Cause and Effect, are not explicitly taught and students are left to figure everything out. I could go on, but I think the point is made. Teaching at the high school level is still in many areas and in many ways largely focused on content without a lot of scaffolding and supports, which are desperately needed by most students, not just ELs.

Trying to change that culture can be really challenging when teachers have large classrooms, perhaps 3 or 4 preps, and are asked to take on additional duties like serve on committees. Introducing new strategies and getting them to change their practice can be really difficult if little time is provided to learn these strategies, and if the time they do have isn't well used or well-structured. Additionally, if the district is trying to introduce too many new concepts at once, teachers will balk, and rightly so!

District leaders need to be sensitive to how much teachers can take in during a year, and understand how to roll out the PD in a way that sustains the learning and doesn't overwhelm the participant. The idea for discussion here is to be very focused and intentional. Choose up to three strategies with which to focus district and school wide, and plan how that will be rolled out to teachers in a way that can be consistently applied. The strategies should be ones that will greatly help all students but especially ELs and SPED students.

When deciding what your focus will be, try to steer away from large general concepts like 'Writing,' or 'Literacy.' Saying that you want all students in the district to improve in writing is fine, but if the people you put in charge of developing the roll out is not intimately familiar with language proficiency levels and other needs of ELs, then the PD might completely miss the mark, or only scratch the surface of what is actually needed.

As an alternative idea, a district could choose unit and lesson planning as its overall focus – using the 'backwards design' approach (starting with the end goal in mind and working forward) which really compels teachers to think about their EL students and how they will scaffold instruction, use pre and post assessments, learning objectives, etc. A year or semester of focused PD on how to plan can be a great beginning to a three-year PD plan.

As you observe your teachers, note the strengths and areas for professional growth and development in the ELD classroom and the depth to which they are planning for and instructing in a way that his seeing positive results. This will be an important consideration for any team building a guiding Blueprint.

Support Professional Development from the ground level

This section outlines general principles you can incorporate into your ESOL blueprint to support teachers, rather than focusing on district PD delivery systems.

As you seek to build a blueprint, I recommend having a series of discussions focused around the extent to which these practices currently exist across your secondary schools. If you find that they are not present, this process of building a blueprint might serve as an opportunity to incorporate a few practices that benefit all students, but are essential for ELs.

The Need for Quality Instruction

Consider the following scenarios I've observed during my career. Do any of them contain any familiar elements?

Scenario A: A new teacher is asked to teach intermediate ELs. No text exists. He is also teaching two other Language Arts classes at different grade levels. This person has to deal with classroom management, establishing relationships and getting to know systems; he must be ahead of his students in all preps, which often requires reading novels ahead of his students. He has very little to no knowledge of ELs or how to effectively teach ELD, let alone differentiate between various levels of language.

Scenario B: An experienced literature teacher is asked to teach ELD. She is given a class of ELL students who speak English fluently, but have not passed the test to exit ELD. These are considered early proficient or 'level 4's'. Not being well versed in ELD, she does what she knows and teaches novels and runs the class like a modified or Sheltered English class with a little more grammar. In essence, the students are taking two English classes.

Scenario C: A teacher is not effective in that she struggles with classroom management, with organization, and with delivery. Lessons begin regularly 20 minutes into the period; students' are off task, not being held accountable to the learning, and no routines or expectations have been established. Students are not achieving and everyone, including her peers is complaining about her inability to teach. The principal decides that the best course of action is to keep her away from the language arts classes and keep her in ELD. Class sizes are smaller there, and it is thought that she will do a little "less damage."

In Scenario A, we see a lack of curriculum, limited classroom management skills, insufficient prep time, and lack of knowledge of ELD. In scenario B, the instructor is an expert in ELA, but lacks knowledge of ELD. Finally, the instructor in Scenario C shows limited classroom management, no routines, and no accountability. Unfortunately, cases like these are fairly common and represent some of the challenges associated with ELD instruction. You'll no doubt recognize some of the challenges that districts face in ELD programming.

Ways to Support Quality Instruction

What is the solution to these common issues? How can the district continue make the best use of its instructors while supporting ELD students? The following are some ideas to improve the experience of both EL students and ELD instructors.

Establish Instructional Routines

I like the saying "Go slow to go fast." What I mean by this is that investing time up front to learn something new can lead to rapid progress later on. You can take the first month of school to establish a set of consistent district- and school-wide instructional routines, which will aid students in the coming months. For example, having all students ask and answer questions in complete sentences, using sentence starters as supports with high academic language, or establishing group roles and behaviors and practicing how to interact independently using academic language in complete sentences with language scaffolds as a support.

Regardless of subject or materials, it's important to establish a set of routines that are done consistently, perhaps daily. The following routines are examples of what one should be seeing in an ELD class daily:

- Structured Partner and Group Interactions (academic conversations): Engage all learners and hold all students accountable to the learning. Students should be speaking in complete sentences and using higher register English.

- Using Sentence/Response Frames to support and build the increased use of academic language.
- Setting Up a Lesson: Learning targets; clearly explaining what the students will be doing; gradual release of responsibility (I do, we do, you do); checking for understanding and holding every student accountable to the learning.
- Engaging and Contextual Vocabulary Routines: Quality reading strategies help students remember their reading. Place high-use vocabulary on a Word Wall and create word webs or graphic organizers, for example.
- Build reading fluency: A variety of reading materials assist students in reading fluency. In echo reading where students repeat what they hear; in choral reading, groups listen and repeat; speed drills, which are fun ways to help students improve automaticity, accuracy, reading rate.
- Extending activities into writing exercises: After students read a text, have them discuss formal language register with scaffolds and then create a piece of writing, such as a summary or formal persuasive essay. Students get used to interacting with text, practice using their academic language, and practice their writing skills consistently.

This list by no means includes everything we would want to see in an ELD class, but they are some of the more essential ones I look for when I'm in classrooms. Regardless of which routines are chosen, when done correctly, students often benefit from consistent, structured routines where they practice using high academic vocabulary, and where they are all held accountable to the learning. Knowing what to expect with these routines provides the added benefit of lowering anxiety, which allows students to participate more fully.

As an example, after observing and looking for sheltered strategies in over 100 classrooms at Salem-Keizer, we found that in classrooms with low student engagement and production, the issues were not about presence of sheltered techniques, but rather about strong classroom management and clear and consistent classroom routines and practices. During group work, for example, many students were either off task, weren't sure what to do or they finished the task quickly and were talking about something else. All were conversing using casual English and many weren't held accountable to the content or developing new vocabulary. We often saw teachers bring the groups back together and call on a couple students at random, or the select few students who were raising their hands. Unfortunately, when this approach is taken too many students can avoid being accountable to the learning. Students are savvy and unless the teacher sets up the activity so that every child is participating and prepared to be called upon, they learn that they can hide. We seldom saw language supports or writing supports, and ELs were not asked to produce much of anything.

In my mind, this really speaks to a lack of consistency around instructional routines and establishing clear expectations in the class early – holding all students accountable. If for example, teachers spent the first month of school establishing group work norms and having students learning how to have academic conversations to a desired effect, then by April and May, the classroom environment would be so much smoother, more focused, and the outcomes would be much greater.

However, building expectations around instructional routines requires commitment from district administration and school administrators as well as professional development and an understanding and buy-in from teachers. In ELD specifically, students need to practice speaking and listening academic English in a structured environment. It's not enough to have a couple kids in a group producing simplistic conversational English. ELP Standards and Common Core State Standards place emphasis on constructing meaning from literary and informational text, and participating in grade-appropriate oral and written exchanges of information, ideas, and analyses, responding to peer, audience, or reader comments and questions. Thus, we need to establish routines that put students into groups and to have them produce language, both oral and written.

I recommend that districts to decide on several key instructional routines that are guided by the goals of the new English Language Proficiency Standards and Common Core State Standards and then provide teachers with a rationale for using them, professional development for implementing them, and accountability for their frequent and consistent usage. Having advocated for meaningful structure and setting up routines, I think it is important to think about the content of the class.

Consider Content

When designing PD I think it is valuable and important to include key aspects of instruction specific to the needs of learning language to ensure that teachers grow and evolve in the areas that help their students the most.

Focus on Critical Content and Long-Term Skills

In ELD classrooms, oftentimes teachers focus on content much like they would in an English Language Arts class, whereas they should be focusing on language *development*. As I received additional professional development and broadened my knowledge base, I began to realize that good teaching is not really about delivering content and 'covering' standards—the so-called "teaching to the test." While covering standards is understandable, quality instruction is about building skills and preparing students for college and career in a rapidly changing world. Simply lecturing on America's Industrial Revolution while students take notes, giving a quiz, and moving on to the next content standard is not the point. A more powerful lesson will challenge the students with activities that provide opportunities to practice long-term skills that can serve them in college and beyond, analyze documents, create an argument and support it with text, create a written response, and practice responses using sentence starters with high academic vocabulary. The former tests their reading and note-taking skills and ability to regurgitate information; the latter teaches them how to think and express themselves on a particular topic. Teaching students how to think, reason and communicate is the point of quality instruction; our ELs require and enjoy the same challenges!

Use Informational text

I was a high school English teacher before I entered the world of administration. I say this with due affection, that we English teachers love our classic novels that unfortunately, too often represent a Eurocentric perspective and experience. In other words, we often fall into the trap of teaching novels that fail to resonate with many of our learners. The truth is that we need to teach a variety of texts from a variety of perspectives - the classic Eurocentric perspective included. Teaching novels is great fun, but it's important to choose books with heroes that reflect different cultures, customs, etc. - especially multi-cultural ones that are engaging and written for modern readers. I remember the year I taught Hosseini's *Kite Runner*: Every student in my classes liked the book and actually read it. I can't say the same about Bronte's, *Jane Eyre*....

While novels are great tools for learning and definitely have a place both in Language Arts and in ELD, equally important is teaching reading, listening, speaking, and writing through expository text. Think about it – the texts our students will encounter in college and in their careers will largely be expository in nature. We need to help ELs prepare for their future by teaching them expository text structure. Additionally, expository text lends itself to high interest, engaging conversations. Part of the goal in ELD is to get students having conversations, practicing the language they are using in a structured environment. This is why in Salem-Keizer I used funds to purchase a monthly magazine with short, high interest articles, into the curriculum. Teachers used close reading strategies to get students talking using structured interactions, and extended their discussions into writing expository responses.

Check for Understanding

I discussed the core value of being results oriented in chapter 1. I would argue that if not all your students are learning the content, then teaching isn't effective. Putting into effect pre-and post-tests and daily or weekly common formative assessments to gauge whether students are learning the content will help provide teachers with the data they need to reteach if necessary. Building on this idea, creating dedicated, well-facilitated teams that are focused on evaluating their data may benefit from these supportive interactions and change practice. Regardless, having a component in your PD of ensuring students are learning the standards being taught is important to include.

Build oral language practices

Our ELs need practice talking, using both conversational and academic English. When students are explaining concepts, they are learning concepts. Additionally, ELs and students living in poverty need practice using *structured* oral language practice – with an emphasis on structured. The old adage my music teachers told me, Practice Makes Perfect, really holds true with learning a language. If we expect students to understand and use a high register of English, then we need to teach them the words and phrases, and give them ample practice until it seems natural. We don't expect our football players to receive a PowerPoint lecture on how to play the game, and then set them loose against another team. We get them on the practice field and we go over plays numerous times until the actions are seamless. Why would we expect anything less from students learning an additional language?

Focus on language for academic purposes

In addition to practicing language frequently and consistently, we need to ensure ELs can comprehend the texts they are asked to read and participate in class discussions, study for tests, and write on what they've learned. Having them 'turn and talk to a neighbor' might be good practice, but unless students are using academic language regularly and with purpose during these interactions, one might question the benefits of these talking opportunities. After all, speaking using the casual language they have mastered won't lead them to possessing a greater command of academic language. As such, ELs need to practice speaking in complete sentences and have sentence frames to help guide them in how to speak and write successfully in that manner. The key here is explicit instruction. Explicit instruction on how to agree and disagree, on how to write a persuasive paragraph, etc.

Actively engage the learner

Like all students, ELs benefit from a curriculum that is high interest and complex, and from structured interactions that are important for language growth. Quality materials that engage and challenge are really important, but students also need to be expected to actively engage and participate in their learning.

When I first began teaching high school English and history, I fondly remember lecturing for 45 minutes, having my students take notes, and then asking for questions during the last few minutes. The three students up front who were asking all the questions appeared to love my lectures, and I'm quite sure I was making a difference in their lives! Yes, I say that tongue and cheek, but that's how I perceived it at the time. I was completely focused on delivering content in a way that I was instructed, and I truly believed I was teaching these kids important information they needed to know. It didn't take long, however, to see that in fact, I was not making a difference. My students were not learning the material and many were bored to tears. A bit of work to actively engage these intelligent minds changed things—for both my students and me!

Require academic rigor

I think one of the myths of working with long-term ELs is the idea that they need material that is less rigorous or demanding. I have found this to be completely false. In fact, ELs who have been in the system for a while need to be pushed academically. We can't make the assumption that they are not smart kids simply because they don't have the language. Teachers can set the bar high as long as they scaffold their lessons and support their students along the way. As stated in the section above about teaching and learning, if the students aren't learning, it's generally not because they can't learn or the material is too complex and difficult. It's because they need more supports. In Salem-Keizer, we are ardent supporters of the teaching method, Gradual Release of Responsibility - the idea that teachers provide some direct instruction, then have students work together to understand the concept being taught before going to independent work. It's during this shared portion that we as instructors are able gauge their ability to understand and if re-teaching the concept is necessary. It's methods like these, as well as other scaffolds, like pointing out key vocabulary, that allows students to grapple with rigorous content. If your ELs are not doing well in a class, avoid the temptation of blaming the learner, and instead look inward.

Allow time to plan lessons

It has been my observation over the years, that one of the great challenges facing teachers is not having enough time to adequately plan lessons that benefit ELs.

ELD teachers do not have the convenience of a bad day: one cannot plan a lesson in the morning after a bad night's sleep. ELD requires one to develop learning goals with both the language and content objectives well ahead-of-time. In other words, you need to know where you are going, what your outcome will be and what resources you need to present the information in multiple ways so that your students will understand the lesson. Additionally, you need to know the linguistic demands of the lesson and how to support different levels of students. This does not happen a half hour before school.

It's important for principals and assistant principals to know how involved ELD is to teach and avoid having those teachers take additional duties, like student activities or government, or coaching, etc. These people need to be treated like specialists, and given ample time to plan and perfect their craft. All teachers need this, true, but ELD teachers and Dual Language teachers have some of the most challenging subjects to teach well. Building time in the week or the day to plan and pull visuals and highlight essential vocabulary is really important.

Therefore, providing a time when an instructional coach and perhaps colleagues teaching the same class can plan together, and review assessment data together can be impactful.

Evaluating Professional Development

At some point, you have to look into the mirror and ask the question: Is it working? Are we making the kinds of progress for our English Learners across the K-12 continuum that is necessary for them to successfully graduate on time and successfully excel in college? Are we focusing on the right professional development that gets at growing a body of educators to truly be effective for ELs? Do our ELs have the kinds of support necessary to be successful?

Make Time to Evaluate

To know the answers to these questions, the district needs to sincerely invest in meaningful and ongoing program evaluation. I will go into the process of evaluating in more depth in chapter 7, but simply put, evaluating the program takes many forms, and can be as simple as surveying various focus groups in the spring of each year, to paying for professionals to come to the district and conduct a formal program evaluation. In Salem-Keizer we do both, but the key to evaluation is to view it as a system-wide inquiry rather than an exercise completed by a few individuals for the sake of completing a state compliance measure.

Evaluating your professional development is not easy because the school year goes so quickly and everyone is incredibly busy throughout the year. However, remember that districts want to have their PD plans for the next year figured out well in advance of the following year, so a good leader will see that the evaluation process is complete in a timely manner and structured in such a way as to inform next steps and allow for budgetary needs and any changes that might involve communication and systematic change. A leader needs to demonstrate the Core Value of Commitment to the Plan in the evaluation process. Yes, you might have many things on your to-do list, but a good leader will plan ahead and delegate tasks to committees. Tasks you will want to plan well ahead and possibly delegate include 1) develop and administer surveys, 2) conduct focus groups, 3) invite in third-party reviewers, and 4) make adjustments to the district's professional development plan. These steps are critical to the evaluation process, but all require focus and intentionality, commitment and time.

ACTIVITY 1: Discussing Professional Development:

As your team engages in different activities related to the creation of an ELE Blueprint, form a group dedicated to planning district-wide professional development. Have this group answer the following questions:

1. Is the focus of professional development geared toward strategies that support disadvantaged learners? (It should benefit all learners, but explicitly support struggling learners including ELs.)
2. Is your plan focused and narrow enough so that teachers don't feel overwhelmed by too many initiatives? Do teachers see the vision and can they see how this plan will benefit their personal growth and the growth of their students?

3. Is your PD delivery plan designed to be effective with adult learners? (Teachers hate having their time wasted)
4. Can this plan be rolled out across several years of implementation?
5. How can teachers be supported so that they feel successful?
6. Do you have the ESOL Department contributing to the design of the PD?
7. Is there a built-in plan for gathering data, evaluating the PD, and adjusting when necessary?

ACTIVITY 2: Leadership Agreements:

Based on reading this chapter, have your Leadership Committee meet and discuss key leadership elements necessary for ensuring schools have the focus and intentionality needed to be successful in educating ELs. Form a short list of leadership priorities and agree to implementing them across schools.

While groups will typically meet to discuss their ideas, I have provided one fun classroom example below as an alternative method for gathering ideas:

Wagon Wheels Brainstorm Facilitation Notes
Developed in the field by educators affiliated with the
National School Reform Faculty

Purposes

- To stimulate lots of generative thinking in a very short time.
- To stimulate powerful thinking between people who might not know each other.
- To create a "vivid image bank" of a new idea in action to inform the planning process.
- To develop a sense of team with a common purpose.

Set up

- Four chairs back to back at the hub of the wheel and four chairs on the outer circle facing the chairs at the hub.
- Facilitator selects four ideas to explore.

Directions

Have participants bring paper and pen and fill in the seats in the wheel(s). Ask them to take notes of both their own ideas as well as their partner's. The people on the outside of the wheel will be moving one seat to the right at each rotation; people at the hub remain in their seats. Explain that they will be working on one topic with each partner for approximately 5 minutes — i.e. they will work with 4 different partners during the activity. For each topic have the participants reach a common understanding of what the topic means and then brainstorm what it would look like in action. At the end of each rotation, ask each participant sitting on the outside of the wheel to rotate one seat to the right. After they settle down, give them the next topic and ask them to reach a common understanding before brainstorming. Next, have participants pick their favorite ideas for each topic and write them down on post-its. Make sure they label the top of each post-it. Put large flip chart sheets with the topic title on the top around the room and have participants post their favorite ideas on the appropriate sheet. Create focus groups to further explore a specific topic and to plan how to put the powerful ideas into action.

CHAPTER 5

English Language Development

Chapter Objectives:

- To build foundational knowledge around ELD
- To identify and support the use of language standards in the ELD classroom.
- To discuss ELD instruction in your district and ensure your system is set up for success.

This chapter discusses English Language Proficiency (ELP) Standards and focuses on the important connection and differences between content standards and ELP-EL programming. Having all teachers understand and reinforce the ELP standards will go a long way to support the language needs in everyday lessons across subjects. Likewise, one cannot overstate the importance of having a curriculum that is relevant and engaging for students, and helpful to teachers.

Standards

When I first began overseeing EL programs in Salem-Keizer, Oregon had a set of standards to be used in English Language Development class, but they were problematic. Although they were good at calling out language functions to focus on, like *distinguish between Cause and Effect*, they looked different from other content standards and therefore, getting teachers in other content areas to use them was a struggle. Furthermore, and more importantly, they were not directly aligned to the annual summative assessment, which understandably caused difficulties in planning and teaching, and for student success!

The new ELPA21 Standards, shared by a consortium of 10 states (Arkansas, Iowa, Kansas, Louisiana, Nebraska, Ohio, Oregon, South Carolina, Washington, and West Virginia), were designed to provide an assessment that would truly measure EL's "mastery of the communication demands of the state's rigorous academic standards." (ELPA21, n.d.b.) Now, for the first time, standards were being created with the intention of providing language proficiency around not only ELD class, but mathematics, science, and English language arts college and career readiness standards, as well.

The effort began in May 2013 when Stanford University's Understanding Language Initiative and the consortium states worked with WestED to create a new set of standards. Since then, 10 ELP standards have been developed that "define what English language skills students should have at particular grade levels. They are designed for collaborative use by both ESL and content-area teachers and address the language demands needed to be successful in English language arts, mathematics, and science classrooms. The ELP Standards are shaped by guiding principles that recognize that ELs have the same potential as native speakers to excel in learning, and that instruction that builds on their varied backgrounds is more likely to help students master their use of the English language." (ELPA21, n.d.b.)

ELPA21 STANDARDS

1. Construct meaning from oral presentations and literary and informational text through grade-appropriate listening, reading, and viewing.
2. Participate in grade-appropriate oral and written exchanges of information, ideas, and analyses, responding to peer, audience, or reader comments and questions
3. Speak and write about grade-appropriate complex literary and informational texts and topics

4. Construct grade-appropriate oral and written claims and support them with reasoning and evidence
5. Conduct research and evaluate and communicate findings to answer questions or solve problems
6. Analyze and critique the arguments of others orally and in writing
7. Adapt language choices to purpose, task, and audience when speaking and writing
8. Determine the meaning of words and phrases in oral presentations and literary and informational text
9. Create clear and coherent grade-appropriate speech and text
10. Make accurate use of standard English to communicate in grade-appropriate speech and writing

As discussed in Chapters 1 and 3, the Castañeda Standard requires educational programs for ELs to be pedagogically sound, which means that they must provide opportunities for ELs to 1) achieve academically in all content areas and 2) learn the oral and written language they need to participate in all content area instruction. There are many different ways that programs can be structured to reach these goals (e.g., bilingual), but all must include attention to content and language standards. Federal and state policies and accountability requirements for ELs, for example, target both content-area standards and English language-development standards. Recall that content standards include Common Core State Standards, Next Generation Science Standards, College and Career-Ready Standards; and ELD standards include ELPA21, and WIDA).

Helping All Teachers Use ELP standards

ELD instruction is specifically targeted to helping EL students use English in an academic context; likewise, ELP standards provide measurable goals to determine how well those students have succeeded.

Initially, as stated previously, ELP standards were designed in isolation of other subject area standards, but in recent years, they have changed to be more closely aligned with the new Common Core State Standards, requiring EL students to produce in a variety of ways across different content areas. With this new, shared responsibility for ELs and the arrival of Common Core State Standards (CCSS) in 46 states and new ELP Standards and assessment systems, it's important to understand the new ELP standards and how they connect with other content areas.

For example, Oregon and 10 other states have adopted 10 ELP standards (ELPA21) for each grade span with connections to math, science, and ELA Common Core Standards. This correlation may seem great on the surface, but teachers may grapple with understanding their content specific standards and may not choose to look at the ELP standards as they prepare lessons unless they are explicitly shown how to do so. The new standards will require changes to how many instructors plan and teach, and these adaptations take patience and time. We need to be supportive, intentional, and proactive to ensure the ELP standards are understood and actually used and referenced in daily lesson plans.

Making Connections between ELP and Common Core State Standards

Given how busy teachers generally are, it's time well spent to 'unpack' the ELP standards to see how they relate to the CCSS and to discuss how they can be added into the lesson planning process. As an example, the following table compares the new ELPA21 Standards used by a ten state consortium to the Common Core standards. Other states use either their own set of standards or the WIDA standards. I provide the ELPA21 standards to simply illustrate how a particular set of standards asks students to produce language and to show the connections with CCSS; this is not an endorsement of a set of standards as being better or more appropriate than another.

The following table shows practices common to four sets of standards: NGSS, CCSS Math, CCSS Reading and Writing, and ELPA21. You can see how common practices, in the cases here, "Determine meaning" and "Interpret meaning" are reflected in these four sets of standards in different subject areas. It is important for all teachers, content and ELD, to realize that the skills students are learning in the specific standards may be able to be applied across multiple content areas.

Shared Practices	NGSS Science Practices	CCSS Math Practices	CCSS Anchor Standards: Reading & Writing	English Language Proficiency 21 Standards
1. Determine Meaning	Ask questions (SP 1)	Make sense of problems and perseverance in solving them (MP 1)	Interpret words and phrases as they are used in a text (R 4)	Determine meaning of words and phrases (ELP 8)
2. Interpret Meaning	Develop and use models (SP 2)	Model with Mathematics (MP 4) Use appropriate tools strategically (MP 5)	Determine central ideas or themes and analyze their development (R 2)	Construct meaning through listening, reading, and viewing (ELP 1)

3. Exchange Information	Obtain, evaluate and communicate information (SP 8)	Attend to precision (MP 6) Reason abstractly and quantitatively (MP 2)	Produce clear and coherent writing appropriate to task (W 4) Develop and strengthen writing as needed (W 5)	Participate in oral and written exchanges of ideas, responses ... questions (ELP 2) Create clear and coherent grade-appropriate speech and text (ELP 9) Accurate use of Standard English (ELP 10)
4. Respond to Complex Texts	Analyze and interpret data (SP 4)	Reason abstractly and quantitatively (MP 2)	Write arguments to support claims / write informative - explanatory texts – complex ideas (W 1 & 2)	Speak and write about complex informational text (ELP 3)

The end goal for this process of comparing ELP standards to state or Common Core Standards is for teachers across the district, but content teachers ideally should make purposeful connections between ELP standards and CCSS. Ideally, ELP standards will be included in all discussions relative to math, science, and ELA standards planning and organization, and all ELD, math, science, and ELA teachers will use ELP standards in their planning.

The process of comparing CCSS and ELP standards, creating supporting documents, and sharing those with teachers can take the better part of a school year. My advice is to bring both the ESOL Department and the Curriculum Department together in September and ask them to take a year to plan, develop, and meet with groups of teachers. Year two would be the implementation year.

Drafting Curriculum and Standards Maps

Generally speaking, curriculum mapping involves identifying standards and aligning the instructional materials, the lessons, the assignments and even the instructional techniques one will use during a course of study. Standards mapping, while included in the curriculum mapping process, can also be a standalone document that identifies which standards will be focused on in each unit of study throughout the course. While similar, it is frequently not viewed as being as comprehensive as a curriculum map. (Curriculum mapping, 2013)

In the past, I have had my team of instructional coaches create standards maps as a pacing guide, to help ELD teachers keep on track throughout the year. We would then bring all ELD teachers together to map out their curriculum using the pacing guide. Based on our old standards, this process made sense and was viewed by teachers as being helpful. With the new ELP standards, however, this work has changed because the new standards more closely mirror the CCSS standards and can be used in every unit. Today we bring teachers together and help them create units that align with standards. Since the new standards can be grouped according to receptive, productive, and interactive modalities, our 'mapping' involves ensuring that a good mixture of these modalities exist in every unit. In this way, we have students listening, speaking, reading and writing in every unit and in many lessons.

We always say that we are firm on the standards but loose on what lessons are used to reach them. This gives teachers the flexibility, creativity and professional latitude to design their own lessons, in keeping with needs of individual students, but it keeps in line with our objectives of teaching the standards through the agreed upon curriculum map.

The creation of a curriculum map will be not only time well spent—it is crucial if teachers are to use the ELP standards to help ELs meet language goals and perform well on the new assessments.

Applying ELP standards Districtwide

In addition to helping individual teachers to incorporate ELP standards into their lessons, I also like to know that instruction based on ELP standards is consistently applied system wide, throughout the district, in both regular and ELD classrooms. This collaboration and shared responsibility allows teams to discuss and plan for rigor and engagement. It provides for student movement across schools, and it helps ELD teachers, who are often a lone teacher of that subject in the school, the ability to plan with others and get ideas, share resources, and receive often-needed support.

The ESOL team may have to draft and prepare documents that explain to district staff how English Language Development differs from Language Arts (discussed later in this chapter). Making this distinction clear will prevent district leadership from focusing erroneously on ELA standards in an ELD classroom and will support the ruling in Lau v. Nichols.

The following are a few steps you can take to enable district-wide use of ELP standards:

- Create guiding documents for all teachers
- Create an implementation plan
- Build sample units and guidance for teachers
- Speak with administrators to build awareness
- Introduce ELP standards to ELD teachers in district PLCs
- Create pilot programs with high schools to build cross-curricular teams that incorporate ELP standards in science and math as well as in ELD.

Promoting Collaborative Understanding and Reinforcement of ELP Standards

While there may be many teachers in a district using Common Core or state standards, there are often only one or two ELD teachers who are using the ELP standards, as mentioned previously. For the rest of the staff, their knowledge of ELD and what goes on in that room can be very limited. Teachers know that ELs need extra support in language and they go to that class for help. That's about the extent of their knowledge for many.

I have always felt that all teachers not only need to know what is being taught in ELD, but they need to know how they can support both teachers with their instruction and students in their learning. You've perhaps heard the saying, "It takes a village," to raise a child. Well, it takes a village to teach ELs properly. As I've stated previously, we need to express the Core Value of shared responsibility and collaboration by supporting what is happening in ELD across all subject areas so that these students can exit that class and be successful in all of their others.

When I was working with all the middle school principals, they asked all staff to reinforce key language functions across the school. When ELD was teaching the language and concepts around Cause and Effect, so was the health class, etc. In some schools, all teachers were required to bring artifacts of student work and display it at each monthly staff meeting. The result was that all teachers learned what's taught in ELD, and they all had ownership of their success. EL students receive a concerted and focused approach to high academic language support across the school, and their data showcases the result.

Remember, the new ELP standards are designed to be shared with other disciplines. These ELP standards should be viewed as a means to help ELs prepare for Common Core, and they should be presented to staff in a way that showcases these standards as companion pieces, not as a separate set of standards. Helping teachers understand how they can be used and the importance of why they must be used in concert with the new CCSS, will go a long way to achieving the desired outcome.

Curriculum

The classroom for monolingual or fluent bilingual speakers is different from the classroom for English Learners. It's important to create units of instruction based on ELP standards, in addition to the content-area standards, and adjust for the needs of students who are learning the English language at differing rates.

The following six principles outlined in the Understanding Language Initiative document, *Key Principles for ELL Instruction* (Stanford University, January 2013), are meant to guide teachers, curriculum leaders, coaches, principals, district administrators, and ESL teachers as they develop units of instruction focused on supporting the language needs of ELs and aligning that to CCSS:

1. Instruction focuses on providing ELLs with opportunities to engage in discipline-specific practices that are designed to build conceptual understanding and language competence in tandem.
2. Instruction leverages ELLs' home language(s), cultural assets, and prior knowledge.

174 · BRAD CAPENER

3. Standards-aligned instruction for ELLs is rigorous, grade-level appropriate, and provides deliberate and appropriate scaffolds.
4. Instruction moves ELLs forward by taking into account their English proficiency level(s) and prior schooling experiences.
5. Instruction fosters ELLs' autonomy by equipping them with the strategies necessary to comprehend and use language in a variety of academic settings.
6. Diagnostic tools and formative assessment practices are employed to measure students' content knowledge, academic language competence, and participation in disciplinary Practices.

However, creating a curriculum from scratch can be challenging for ELD teachers. Instructors face a number of hurdles when learning to teach ELD: understanding proficiency levels, understanding how to teach language to ensure proficiency growth, how to establish routines for grouping and speaking, understanding the difference between ELA and ELD, accountability, and so on. To expect teachers to overcome these hurdles and create their own ELD curriculum is a high expectation, even with an hour of prep time each day. New ELD teachers come in all of the time, resulting in inconsistent instruction and differing rigor and engagement from classroom to classroom.

How can leadership provide a solution? I suggest that the district invest in a strong engaging ELD curriculum—a textbook with planning guides and support videos, etc.—is really important for consistency of instruction across the district and as an essential support to new teachers. ELD is a hard class to teach even for the veterans. So much time goes into the planning process, and when one has several preps, which is often the case in larger class sizes, we need to make it easier for our teachers, not harder. An ELD curriculum will make that challenge a bit easier by giving the teacher a place to begin without precluding creation of unique units.

Choosing a District-wide Curriculum

In the past, I've been asked two key questions pertaining to choosing a curriculum. The first is how I determine what kind of curriculum is needed. After talking with ELD teachers in a district professional learning community forum, it became clear that instructional materials are in fact, desired and necessary; that the materials are engaging to their students, and appropriate for their age levels.

Our teachers had textbooks they kept on the shelf because their students were bored, and at times felt insulted by the examples used. Teachers asked for on-line support materials, visuals, and short videos. They asked for common formative assessments, summative assessments and materials already aligned with standards. They asked for relevant, engaging topics that would inspire discussion and debate. So, when we piloted materials from various companies, those were some of the criteria we were looking at in determining if it met our needs.

The second question I received focused on leadership. What does a leader do implement choosing a curriculum? Well, as outlined above, I brought them all together. I surveyed them and listened. I looked at the materials and had them show me examples of what they found boring, or ineffective. Afterwards, I tasked a person with reaching out to publishers to pilot their materials. We told them what we were looking for and had them come and give a formal presentation. We included a few of our teachers in the presentation, and asked several to pilot the materials and give formal feedback. Later in the year, we came together as a group. We looked at their assessments and listened to their evaluations. Then we had others try the same piloted materials to see if they agreed and felt the same way about them. Once we had most if not all of the teachers excited about a set of materials, we purchased them. It was an involved process having community members and students providing input in addition to the teachers. The results, however, were that teachers felt supported and that they had the tools to teach effectively. We saw engaging lessons and students focused on achieving on standards. We saw students progressing.

Characteristics of ELD curricula

You'll want to ensure all ELD levels have a different curriculum that is aligned with CCSS. Also, be sure that teachers align new ELP standards with CCSS and plan curriculum using these standards.

When I look at ELD instructional materials, I want to make sure, that at minimum, two goals are accomplished: First, that teachers should be excited about the materials and feel they are very helpful to teaching and reaching their objectives.

Second, the materials should be engaging to the learner! Students should be motivated to talk about what they are reading and studying. In ELD, I want to see groups of students having lively conversations using a high academic language register, as part of the lesson. If you can't get them to have fun talking, then ELD is going to be a long year.

I also look for materials that include instructional routines. As an example, Scholastic's English 3D incorporates daily routines that get kids used to doing language warm ups at the beginning of class each day. We find that so much about successful language practice comes with establishing small group discussion routines early and often. Having instructional materials that have good routines included for this purpose can be a benefit.

Finally, I like my ELD classes to be guided by the ELP standards and for teachers to plan their units with these at the forefront.

Curriculum options

There are a number of ELD curricula on the market with different characteristics. Different high school ELD curriculum options that were explored in

SK include Scholastic Action, English 3D, and The Edge. We invested time into exploring these products due to their engaging and relevant nature and based on our goals.

Creating District Cohesiveness in Curriculum

Regardless of whether you purchase and ELD curriculum or create your own, I've found that it's important to have consistency in curriculum across district high school ELD classrooms Just as with ELD standards. Curriculum consistency will provide support to teachers through district PLC planning times and ensure common practice, and reliable materials and routines. In order to provide this cohesiveness, there are some steps you can take.

I've found that the best way to produce a unified front with regards to curriculum is to make the most out of your Professional Learning Communities (PLCs). There are number of ways you can use PLCs. Although teachers have PLC time at their schools, we also offer a district-wide PLC that brings all ELD teachers together with their instructional coaches. Part of the day is receiving professional development and half of the day is spent planning units by language levels. This is really helpful for all ELD teachers but especially for those who are alone at their school with no one to collaborate with. It also builds a sense of team and allows for establishing common agreements on standards, on material usage, on common formative assessments, routines, data protocols, etc.

We found that piloting new ELD materials and engaging kids and getting them actively involved was a lot easier to understand and plan as a group in these settings.

Evaluation of Curriculum Efficacy

As with any aspect of the blueprint, curriculum is subject to evaluation. When evaluating a curriculum, you can observe classrooms that are using the new curriculum to evaluate lesson plan design, implementation of key strategies, connections with standards, and rigor and relevance. These observations can also be used to learn how to support instructors. Finally, pre- and post-tests for each ELD curriculum unit can reveal a lot about how it's working overall. If you did not hit the target, what adjustments can you make so ensure my students learned the concept or vocabulary.

ELD Instruction

While 'sheltered' instruction (described in chapter 6) uses *language* to teach *content*, remember and that ELD involves using *content* to teach *language*. As stated in this quote from Saunders, et al., 2013:

> *English Language Development (ELD) instruction is designed specifically to advance English learners' knowledge and use of English in increasingly sophisticated ways. In the context of the larger effort to help English learners succeed in school, ELD instruction is designed to help them learn and acquire English to a level of proficiency (e.g., advanced) that maximizes their capacity to engage successfully in academic studies taught in English. (p. 14)*

At the secondary level, ELD is typically a separate stand-alone class that is aligned with your state ELP standards. Instruction should focus on both academic and conversational English, and it should focus on the English vocabulary, syntax, functions, conventions, and morphology. Finally, the class should "integrate meaning and communication to support explicit teaching of language." (Saunders et.al.)

Some ELD classes focus on grammar with students filling in handouts and being drilled in verb usage, or the like; however, these are *not* ideal ELD classes: Classes should be communicative in nature, engaging students in academic conversations using the forms and functions of language in a purposeful way, and frequently extending those conversations into writing. Be cautious about grouping for the sake of interaction alone, however, as having students talk to one another periodically in a casual way will usually not end in a desired growth of academic language production ability.

ELD v English Language Arts

We now come to address one of the most important things about ELD: the distinction between ELD class and English Language Arts (ELA). ELA teachers are often asked to teach ELD and they often have limited knowledge about how the two classes differ, and how they need to change their instruction to address the needs of ELs. Additionally, and just as importantly, administrators need to understand the differences in order to advocate and guide the ELD teachers in their schools.

So what are the differences? Put in simple terms, English language arts is focused on teaching the content standards of English. It's a class designed for students to develop skills in reading literature and providing literary analysis; on understanding plot structures and author's purpose, or point of view, or tone. It's a class designed for developing their writing skills and being able to articulate themselves using various forms of writing, e.g. persuasive, narrative, expository, and so on.

ELD, on the other hand, is a *language* class meant to strengthen the linguistic skills of a student and serve as a bridge to their academic success. Classes are divided by language proficiency levels, and focus on language standards, rather than content standards; teachers focus on providing explicit language instruction – instruction students have had very little exposure to, but that's used in text books where students are expected to both understand and produce successfully.

The available evidence suggests that ELD instruction should explicitly teach, and engage students in consciously studying, the elements of the English language as applicable to both academic and conversational language, with significant time devoted to speaking and listening, and particular attention to meaning and communication. (Saunders et. al., (2013)

While the goals of the two classes are very different, ELD classes often wrongly end up resembling ELA class, but with more grammar or vocabulary exercises added. I've been to many ELD classrooms where students were reading novels and discussing themes or characterization using informal, conversational language – with the teacher calling on one or two students to tell the class what they think about a particular character or passage. This approach to teaching a novel, while it *might* be appropriate for ELA, or seen as engaging, is not what one would expect to see in a class focused on language acquisition. Properly executed, ELA and ELD will look different, even if they are using the same material.

In ELD, for example, the teacher should be focused on language that will be taught and reinforced in structured dialogue. Key vocabulary words will have to be identified prior to reading a chapter. A mini lesson, perhaps on theme or another literary device, would have to be taught and clearly understood prior to reading. The thing to think about when teaching a novel, is how much time will be spent on this assignment and what English Language Proficiency Standards will be addressed?

The point I'm trying to get across is that ELD is about language. Spending three weeks on any assignment that doesn't clearly build a student's academic language or deepen their ability in other ELP standards can waste precious time that's needed to promote English Language proficiency. To be clear, it is not that I think novels shouldn't be taught. A teacher can have students participate in close reading activities, have several key standards identified, and have great meaningful (and structured) conversations around a book that perhaps really connects with their lives; but it really needs to be structured for academic language growth.

ELD teachers need to think in terms of urgency - what gaps do my students have, and how can I give them the language they need to be successful in school? This is a very different focus from a standard English language arts class.

ACTIVITY: Gallery Walk

The objective of this activity is to understand how ELD is functioning in your district and what improvements are needed to ensure teachers feel supported and students feel engaged and successful in their pursuits to acquire conversational and academic English. The Gallery Walk strategy is one I use with teachers to generate good discussions and planning.

(Note: Your Leadership team may decide to go out into ELD classrooms to observe, and/or bring in instructional coaches if you have them, and several ELD teachers to lend to the discussion.)

Gallery Walk Described -

(I borrowed this idea from Engage NY)

What is a Gallery Walk? A "Gallery Walk" is an activity that allows participants/students to discuss and display their final work around a room much like artists would display their artistic pieces in an "exhibit." It is a way that participants/students can share their group work projects or individual literary responses to a text in a non-threatening way with the assurance of getting some feedback from their learning community.

When do I implement a Gallery Walk, and what specifics steps would I take to implement it?

A "Gallery Walk" Activity can be used to share collaborative group work in the classroom in the following way:

1. It can be used to "exhibit" collaborative group posters around the classroom, as a culminating activity. a. An assigned task/activity is completed by a team of 4-6 students that form Home Base Teams.

b. When the Home Base Teams finish their collaborative work poster, the teacher displays each group's final work around the classroom.

c. Then the teacher informs the Home Base Teams that they will visit each one of the posters to generate a discussion about their peer's work/ poster with their immediate group, as well as to make comments and/or post Clarifying Questions using post-its.

d. Once each of the Home Base Teams has visited each of the posters, the Home Base Teams return to their work table/station.

e. The teacher then collects any clarifying questions that were posted on the posters with post-its and commences a Whole Group Discussion.

f. Each clarifying question is directed to the collaborative group that generated and/or created the poster. To facilitate the discussion, the teacher reads each clarifying question and then writes them on a white board/smart board/chart paper, identifying each question by Home Base Team numbers (i.e., Group 1, 2 or by the Groups invented name, if appropriate)

g. Then a discussion ensues; the facilitator/teacher gives each Home Base Team the floor when their question is brought up. The Home Base Team is afforded the opportunity to answer the clarifying question, which can be done by one representative from the group or by all the group members chiming in when appropriate and/or there is a pause after a team member adds a final comment.

CHAPTER 6

Content

Chapter Objectives:

- To discuss how content teachers are supporting ELs for their success.
- To build foundational knowledge around 'Sheltered' instruction and Primary Language Support.

I am including a chapter on content instruction because the success of English learners, as I've stated previously, cannot fall to the ELD teacher alone. Their success lies in the entire school planning and thinking about how to focus on and support language growth, how to challenge and inspire them to achieve, and attend to their emotional well-being. Think of them as valued members of your family who require some additional support to be and feel accepted and successful.

Content Area Instruction

The way core content is planned and taught is vitally important to EL success. ELs typically have one period of ELD per day, with the remaining five or six periods in regular core content classes. But what is that experience like for EL students? Are they getting the material taught to them in a way that they can comprehend? Do they know what the lesson is about and what they are supposed to do? Did they understand the instructions? Are they allowed to practice with a peer and given a chance to ask questions in a way that feels safe before having to produce a product or provide an answer? Investing time in professional development that allows for teachers to plan and instruct in this way, and to assess to see if they are being successful and if not, having the time to re-teach, is really critical. If we believe all students will achieve the standards, then we have to make sure all students can actually reach the standards. This goes back to my core value of Being Results Oriented. Is every student held to the same expectations and standards? If not, what kinds of supports are needed to ensure they can get results?

Content Standards

Every teacher is familiar with content area standards. They hit subjects such as science, math, language arts, as well as many other subject areas. They are designed ensure high achievement and they provide teachers with a clear idea of what knowledge and skills our students need in every grade level.

While commonly used today, they were first included in the 1994 reauthorization of the Elementary and Secondary Education Act (ESEA), by the Clinton administration, and carried forward by subsequent administrations and their reauthorizations of ESEA.

Content standards, like Common Core and Next Generation Science, are important to for all students including English Learners, because they spend the majority of their day in content area classrooms and they are trying to master not only the academic language acquisition and practices used throughout school, but the social language too. As stated in an article by Staehr, D., & Segota, J., titled "Standards that Impact English Language Learners,"

> Standards provide a tool for defining the language as well as the content that ELLs are expected to achieve. In order for ELLs to succeed academically in US schools, both ELP standards and professional teaching standards for English as a second language (ESL) teachers are needed to ensure achievement for ELLs.

The reason I like the Common Core Standards for EL's is due to the fact that students are required to produce language and writing. When followed correctly, students are no longer passive learners, but actively demonstrating their learning in multiple ways.

With the right language supports and routines in place, and with the understanding of proficiency levels and what ELs can produce at various stages, teachers have the ability to help their EL students successfully reach the standards, and that is exciting!

Sheltered Instruction in the Content Classroom

When we talk about core content and content standards, we need to recognize how difficult it is to be in a class that is taught in a foreign language. Anyone working with ELs in a meaningful way (trying to ensure they are successfully learning the content) understands the need to adjust their instruction so that their ELs can keep up with the rest of the class. I've often thought that if you dumped me in China and asked me to learn science and do well on exams I would need a whole lot of visual support. I would need key vocabulary identified, and I'd sure appreciate it if the teacher didn't speak really fast and if I could work in small groups with others who could help me. Even then I'd be struggling!

According to one definition provided by the Northwest Regional Education Service District (ESD), "Sheltered instruction is a set of teaching strategies, designed for teachers of academic content, that lower the linguistic demand of the lesson without compromising the integrity or rigor of the subject matter." Sheltered instruction, therefore, places more emphasis on *language* as a vehicle to reach instructional and assessment goals centered around *content*.

There are several methods you can use to relay academic content to EL students. "Teachers adjust the language demands of the lesson in many ways, such as modifying speech rate and tone, using context clues and models extensively, relating instruction to student experience, adapting the language of texts or tasks, and using certain methods familiar to language teachers (e.g., demonstrations, visuals, graphic organizers, or cooperative work) to make academic instruction more accessible to students of different English proficiency levels." (Best Practices for ELs, n.d.)

Sheltered Instruction vs. Sheltered Classrooms

When discussing EL instruction, it is important to recognize and distinguish between the terms *sheltered instruction* and *sheltered classrooms*. Sheltered instruction is a teaching *method* - one that I would hope to see spread across content area classrooms in all schools. A sheltered classroom by contrast, is a class designed expressly for English Learners. For students new to the country and with very varying degrees of literacy in their native language, for example, we provide a sheltered history or science class that offers elective credit. This class is designed to teach content, but at a slower pace and with a focus on building language. While sheltered classrooms can be very helpful for beginning ELs, we need to be careful to not have them for intermediate learners. Having a system of sheltered classrooms can lower expectations, track whole groups of students, adversely affect their self-esteem, and prevent them from getting core credits in high school to graduate. A better course of action, I believe, is to have intermediate ELs in regular classes, and ensure they are with teachers who have been properly trained and are using sheltered techniques: building background, making the content comprehensible, using scaffolding techniques and language objectives, considering proficiency levels in their planning and assessments, etc.

Taking the time to ensure several teachers in each grade level and in each subject area are provided PD relative to how one incorporates language into content lessons, and then purposefully placing your ELs in their classes to the best of your ability, is not only smart, but the right thing to do. After all, placing ELs in a person's class who teaches in a very traditional manner (lecture and note taking, etc.), and doesn't use sheltered techniques, can be similar to throwing a non-swimmer into the deep end of a pool. Some will learn to swim to the side, sure, but most of the others will sink. Better to take the extra effort in placing students properly as you work with your staff to grow their abilities in supporting all students.

When I first came to Salem-Keizer, we had high school students at all language levels in sheltered classrooms. I often found that the rigor was missing in those core classes and the expectations were lower based on the fact that the standards were either not followed or they were modified. Students weren't challenged in many cases, and many were often bored, uninspired, and some discussed feeling 'stupid.' Furthermore, teaching these students were often viewed by other teachers as being the responsibility of the 'sheltered' teacher or the ELD teacher, rather than a shared responsibility among the staff. Additionally, many teachers commented that ELs would never do well outside of a sheltered environment because they needed the extra support.

I felt that that structure was not beneficial to our intermediate to intermediate high students (Language levels 3 and 4). Based on my and my team's observations and both the anecdotal, informal and formal data we collected showing that our growth was not improving at Salem-Keizer, we decided to offer our ELs sheltered support in core classes, and dismantle the majority of our sheltered classrooms. Our mantra was, 'challenge but support.'

We placed ELs in mainstream classes with sheltered instruction because we want students to be taught consistently from middle school to high school. We also want them to have high expectations placed on them and access to rigorous CCSS curriculum, and we want them mixed in with non-EL students. The changes were difficult for some at first, mostly because some feared that students would suffer without being in a series of support classes. Over time, however, the culture changed and teachers saw that EL students were making it - albeit with language supports - and we have seen more teachers expressing an interest in finding strategies to support ELs.

While a lot more work is needed to ensure their academic success, we believe our efforts are making a difference and moving in a very positive way. Designing a blueprint necessitates a pedagogically sound approach when it comes to instruction in core content classes. It requires careful planning and focused agreement on what instructional strategies are necessary for teachers to use so that ELs are successful. No one program or approach is going to serve as a magic bullet, but helping EL students access the material is necessary for their success.

Primary Language Instruction

"Learning a second language is a long and complex undertaking. Your whole person is affected as you struggle to reach beyond the confines of your first language and into a new language, a new culture and a new way of thinking, feeling and acting." (Brown, D., 2014, p. XX)

A strategy that has been historically overlooked, downplayed, or received poorly in the United States is the idea of using a child's primary language to help him or her acquire English. There have been times in our history when bilingualism was more accepted and even promoted in some schools. For example, it was common to see bilingual classrooms using German prior to the First World War. But other forces in the U.S. connected the English language to patriotism, which created issues for bilingual education. (Goldenberg, 2015)

The argument of immersing a child in English Only remains popular, in fact, and was reinforced in the No Child Left Behind law (2002), a reauthorization of the Elementary and Secondary Education Act (ESEA, 1965). This law did not stop or prevent bilingual programs from existing, but it "imposed a high-stakes testing system that promoted the adoption and implementation of English-only instruction. Furthermore, all references to bilingual education in the previous ESEA were eliminated in the new legislation" (Nieto, D. 2009, p. 64).

Additionally, an English Only movement became popular starting in the 1990's when several states (California, Arizona and Massachusetts) led by California's Proposition 227, passed laws preventing bilingual education. The supporters of Proposition 227 maintained that, "poor academic performance of Spanish speakers was due to their placement in bilingual programs, and promised that these students would have superior academic outcomes if placed in English-only programs." (Gandara, Para. 8., 2015)

With years of data now in place, we can see the adverse effects this movement has had on English Learners and that the promised "superior academic outcomes" never materialized. A series of studies published in *Forbidden Language: English Learners and Restrictive Language Policies*, in 2011 supported this observation. The studies showed that the achievement gaps for these students did not close; in fact, ELs had greater dropout rates and increased placement into special education classrooms. Additionally, each state saw a decline of qualified bilingual teachers by as much as 50%. (Gandara, P., & Hopkins, M., 2010)

Since that time, a growing body of research demonstrates that English Learners achieve in learning English when they are able to use of all their linguistic resources. As David Nieto (2009) writes:)

> …children with limited English proficiency who are taught using at least some of their native language perform significantly better on standardized tests than similar children who are taught only in English. This conclusion was based on the statistical combination of eleven studies. These studies were selected for the quality of their research design from a total of seventy-five studies reviewed. They included standardized test score results from 2,719 students in thirteen different states, 1,562 of whom were enrolled in bilingual programs. Further studies show that providing instruction in the students' native languages does not only facilitate English acquisition but also strengthens content knowledge attainment (p. 65)

Many readers of this book may not have the means to create a robust offering of bilingual programs and will instead rely on developing their ELE programs. While ELE programs can be successful without the intentional use of primary language support, the bulk of the studies of bilingual education show that primary language instruction produces better results in terms of English achievement (in addition to improved achievement in students' first language) compared to all-English immersion. At a minimum, students in bilingual programs achieve in English at the same levels as children in all-English instruction, but with the added advantage of superior achievement in their home languages, thus a net advantage for bilingual education.

I cannot express how rewarding it is to watch my Spanish speaking preschool students come to school during the first week in September and see them immediately engage in learning in their native language. The messages they receive when they can express themselves and share their stories and experiences in their own language in their own language to their teachers, is extremely valuable. After all, if I entered school and no one spoke my language and my teacher didn't know my language or my culture, I'd feel a little awkward, to say the least. A district that recognizes the value of the student's primary language demonstrates the Core Value of Continuity of Care in that it reinforces positive messages that primary language proficiency is an asset to be nurtured, not a liability.

As highlighted in chapter 1 Core Value #4, Dr. Escamilla has partnered with Salem-Keizer as one of its research districts for the implementation of Literacy Squared – an approach to instruction that seeks to develop bilingualism and biliteracy in Spanish speaking students in the elementary years. The data collected across 13 elementary schools showed that students who had instruction using this method outperformed both the state and the district's English learners not in Literacy Squared, on the state's reading assessment in the 4th and 5th grade.

While this research focuses on our elementary schools, I think it is important for secondary educators in that developing strong bilingual pathways has the potential to decrease long-term ELs, prevent dropouts and thus increase graduation rates.

As mentioned above, building bilingual pathways to help students acquire two languages to proficiency—ideally from Kindergarten through 12th grade can be beneficial and time well-spent. That said, it's important to remember that no one program or approach is a panacea in solving the achievement gap or getting kids to graduate on time and be prepared for college and career. Merely having a program does not equal success. Creating a successful, vibrant program requires strong and aligned systems related to assessment, curriculum, instruction, staff quality, professional development, community building, program structure, and resources. It takes time and a lot of support from the district. In other words, it is not something to do half-heartedly. As the coordinator of a Two Way Immersion program for secondary schools, I can tell you that it takes considerable time and energy to be effective. Having said that, the time invested in growing a bilingual program, even if it begins with one teacher in one grade level and grows from year-to-year, is well worth the effort.

ACTIVITY: How to Build Language Supports into Content Classrooms Across the District using Chalk Talk

Like the title states, the goal of this activity is to generate ideas around how to ensure ELs are getting the language supports they need in all classrooms, not just in ELD. I have chosen Chalk Talk because it allows for reflection and generating ideas in a quiet, inclusive way.

Chalk Talk Described:

Originally developed by Hilton Smith, Foxfire Fund; adapted for the NSRF by Marylyn Wentworth.

Chalk Talk is a silent way to do reflection, generate ideas, check on learning, develop projects or solve problems. It can be used productively with any group—students, faculty, workshop participants, committees. Because is it done completely in silence, it gives groups a change of pace and encourages thoughtful contemplation. It can be an unforgettable experience. Middle Level students absolutely love it—it's the quietest they'll ever be!

Format Time: Varies according to need; can be from 5 minutes to an hour. Materials: Chalk board and chalk or paper roll on the wall and markers.

Process 1. The facilitator explains VERY BRIEFLY that chalk talk is a silent activity. No one may talk at all and anyone may add to the chalk talk as they please. You can comment on other people's ideas simply by drawing a connecting line to the comment. It can also be very effective to say nothing at all except to put finger to lips in a gesture of silence and simply begin with #2.

1. The facilitator writes a relevant question in a circle on the board. Sample questions:

- What ideas expressed in this chapter are not evident in our current professional development plan?
- How would you improve our PD plan so that ELs and other disadvantaged youth were better represented?
- What did you learn today?
- So What? or Now What?

3. The facilitator either hands a piece of chalk or a marker to everyone, or places many pieces of chalk at the board and hands several pieces to people at random.

4. People write as they feel moved. There are likely to be long silences—that is natural, so allow plenty of wait time before deciding it is over.

5. How the facilitator chooses to interact with the Chalk Talk influences its outcome. The facilitator can stand back and let it unfold or expand thinking by:

- circling other interesting ideas, thereby inviting comments to broaden
- writing questions about a participant comment

CHAPTER 7

Program Evaluation

Chapter Objective:

- To discuss the importance of ongoing evaluations and working that process into your yearly planning cycle

The Importance of Ongoing Evaluation

One of the keys to any blueprint planning is the idea of evaluation. Simply put, how do you know that your efforts - whether that be in the classroom or implementing components of the blueprint - is making a difference?

I once had a principal look at the blueprint documents I was presenting to him and asked, "How do I know that we're being successful and hitting the target?" It was a great question! Truly, how do you know when you are making a difference and that your ELs are closing the achievement gap? *Evaluation,* defined by Merriam Webster as, "to judge the value or condition of something in a careful and thoughtful way." The Castaneda Standard demands demonstrable results, and the category of evaluation is a key part of determining how well you serve your EL population. It also expresses the Core Value in chapter one, of being Results Oriented.

The category of evaluation is vitally important to my team of instructional coaches because we always want to know whether we are making an impact and truly helping students.

This chapter looks at the importance of evaluations and divides the topic into three categories: classroom, school, and the ELE Program as a whole. To not continually evaluate and seek input from multiple stakeholders about what is working well and not working as planned, is to not truly be involved in the improvement process.

ELD Classroom-based Evaluation

It goes without saying that your instructors are key to building a solid ELD program. While all teachers share in the responsibility of educating ELs and should also be constantly evaluating and looking for results, I focus on the district's ELD staff as a great place to begin. The district ELD staff is smaller, more manageable, and easier to bring together and support. After all, if we want our ELs to grow in their use of academic language, we need to be sure that our language teaching staff have a solid understanding as to how to teach the class and to see that their efforts are having an impact on language growth.

In working with secondary ELD teachers over the years, I cannot tell you how often we observed teachers teaching units but never measuring their success. I have seen teachers not really understanding their students proficiency levels and not having clear goals as to where they need to take them. Teaching a language lesson is really not difficult and in going to observe a language class, you most likely will see that teaching language is occurring in some form. But how do we know *what* language needs to be acquired? How do we know that a new intermediate language level student is steadily progressing to upper intermediate? Do ELD teachers have a plan, are the following a standards map, and are they assessing students constantly along the way to gauge whether they are being successful and needing to loop back and re-teach?

I feel compelled to say that I have seen many great examples of strong planning, instruction, and evaluation in ELD classes throughout the years too. However, my point here is to suggest that effectively teaching ELD is difficult and it requires purposeful and intentional district coordination and support.

ELD teachers come and go and many have very little experience in teaching language. Some are brand new teachers just trying to figure out classroom management while taking on several preps and perhaps an extra duty or two because the principal asked them to do so, and they felt obligated. If ELs are to be successful and progress linguistically each year, they must have a strong foundation ELD instruction (as well as support across subject areas).

In supporting ELD teachers across the district, I want every one of them to know they are not alone - that they are part of a larger team. I want them to know they have support and can reach out for help. I want them to know that we have a district vision (blueprint) and how they fit into that vision.

In supporting my ELD teachers, I tasked my program assistant and team of my coaches with the following activities that would promote self-reflection and evaluation:

District-wide Professional Learning Communities: We brought all ELD teachers together three times a year for an entire day. The first half of the day might consist of new learning, to reinforce the best practices of ELD, introduce new strategies or routines, and creating or agreeing to a standards map, etc. The afternoon then, would bring all like proficiency level teachers together to create units and common formative assessments with an instructional coach. These efforts were powerful in that we became a strong district team of ELD staff.

These efforts also resulted in having all ELD teachers give what is called The Gap Finder - an informal language assessment to see where the gaps in language exist - so that teachers could focus on those gaps. It got all ELD staff thinking and looking at their students' summative assessment strand data in reading, writing, listening, and speaking. All ELD staff spent time writing common formative assessments for the units they created with their peers and with coaches. In our PLC's when we were creating our common formative assessments, we stressed the importance of evaluation and monitoring growth, and we outlined which standards to focus on so that everyone was on the same page, so-to-speak.

We also initiated a series of instructional rounds, which took half of them into the other half's classrooms to observe for certain pre-determined student learning examples, and then we switched and had the other half go and do the same. The conversations afterwards were very rich and the teachers felt good about getting out of their classrooms and being able to visit others.

We provided an observation tool specifically for ELD classrooms and had all teacher agree to two aspects of the tool to focus on. Then we had coaches go and observe their lessons (as best we could with limited staff) and provide coaching feedback on those elements in a safe, non-evaluative way.

All of these efforts were initiated around the idea of evaluation: how do we know we are making a difference and that students are learning and progressing in language proficiency?

School-based Evaluation

I began this chapter at the classroom level because the classroom is ultimately where the learning needs to take place. If ELD teachers do not have a strong sense of where their students are linguistically, and unsure how to, or whether they are moving them to the next level, then we have a problem. If content teachers aren't adjusting their planning and instruction to meet the needs of their most vulnerable learners, then we also have a problem.

Having a strong team of ELD teachers -- and ensuring that all teachers are together in setting goals and moving forward in supporting ELs -- takes significant coordination and planning. In considering evaluation then, the next natural place to focus one's efforts is at the school level.

Title IA schools are already familiar with the evaluation process because they must do a lot of planning in order to receive their title dollars; non-title schools, perhaps not as much or to the same extent. Regardless, the process of looking at your school and gauging how effective it is in serving its most vul-

198 · BRAD CAPENER

nerable students is an important exercise, and one that I'm going to briefly describe in this section.

Before I address the initial components of school evaluation, can we agree that implementing any kind of substantive change at a school - especially change that is viewed as a departure from current and past practice - comes with myriad challenges, and potential pitfalls? Principals may or may not have experience in leading a staff to embrace lasting change, or culture change, but regardless of their experience, I think it is extremely important for them to have significant support from the district office. Exhibiting overt support to principals is empowering and allows a good leader to make important changes that may disrupt the status quo, without fearing that his or her job is at stake. Of course, going in a particular new direction needs to be well communicated and supported by the superintendent, but support is a condition that needs to be in place so that leaders can do what they are paid to do. This might seem like an obvious statement, but I have talked with principals who have commented to me that they do not feel supported, and therefore, are hesitant to do anything that will appear too disruptive.

Now, assuming the leadership component is in place, principals need to have a good grasp of where they are strong instructionally and where they need to improve. To do this, several pieces of the puzzle need to be in place:

Support from Staff: Changing the culture of a school or making adjustments to instructional components, require a team, not a person. In other words, if change is going to be realized and supported over time, it needs to have strong support from staff. After all, leaders come and go, and the school needs to continue building a strong culture that supports all students. Having said that, I think it is important to have a committee of involved teachers - several of whom are influential - to help create a plan of improvement that can be supported.

Data Gathering and Analysis: Next, you need to have good data that shows where the strengths and weaknesses exist. To do this, many schools conduct a

Needs Assessment. In Salem-Keizer, we distributed Needs Assessments, surveys, and have looked at summative data to compare various sub-group outcomes to the whole school. We also developed an observation tool with Dr. Claude Goldenberg and Dr. Ilana Umansky, that was created to assist principals identify those areas of need. We found that having an outside group come and spend a day observing multiple classrooms using a valid and reliable tool grounded in research, was helpful to the principal and his/her team in affirming the instructional areas they already believed were in need of improvement. Furthermore, it assisted principals in having quality conversations with staff about the need for change.

While creating an observation tool to help inform school strengths and areas of need is great, not everyone has the resources or time to invest in such in-depth work. At the classroom level, however, multiple observation walk-through tools exist and perhaps your district already uses one. The thing to remember is that it has to be focused in part on improving conditions for English Learners. I remember a time when my district rolled out the broad use of an observation walkthrough tool that all high school administrators were to use, but it had no indicators dealing with sheltered strategies - or strategies intended to help ELs access the content; it contained nothing that would help administrators have conversations with teachers about creating or improving a learning environment for English Learners. This was alarming at first because we have the largest EL population in the state and it's hard to improve conditions in classrooms if administrators and teachers are not having regular and ongoing conversations about improving results and ensuring all students are reaching the standards. We did ultimately amend the tool and worked with district staff to use the combined one instead, but it served as a lesson for the need to have shared vision in goal setting, as I describe below.

Goal setting: Once your data has been collected, the key is to choose a limited number of areas with which to focus. You may, for example, identify five to seven areas of need, but your staff is only going to be able to focus on a couple areas a year. I can't stress enough the importance of not placing too much on your staff. Allow them to focus on a couple areas each year and help them see the big picture and how they are reaching those goals. Your teachers should know that a guiding blueprint exists and understand their role in the vision.

As to the goals that you identify, make sure they are shared and articulated across departments and teams; make sure they are measurable, achievable, and timely. It is also advisable to divide the goals into phases and spread them over several years. This way, you can monitor your progress and adjust as necessary while keeping the team focused on the overall goals of the program.

Review and adjust: In the beginning of each year, I lead several teams through a goal setting exercise. We meet to review our goals from the previous year and then write new ones. As the year progresses, we typically meet monthly to discuss our goals, look at data, and make adjustments. Finally, again in the spring we come together to review our progress and bring evidence to show to see how close we came to achieving our goals. The key here is to go through the process of reviewing goals, having honest conversations, and making adjustments. Each school leader is going to want to have their own process and timeline for evaluating the goals they are working on, but the point is to use an evaluation process.

Engage stakeholders: Often times we are asked to create plans and get them approved so that funding can occur. Principals feel pressure to write plans and submit the necessary language to receive their funding. The point of including stakeholders in the planning, however, is really critical. It's critical because it's a reality check. We might be involved in a lot of activities to improve instruction, but how are students feeling about the experience, and what input can they provide the in the learning process? Parents too are the ones helping students at home with homework, and they perhaps have some insight as to how things can improve. Community groups often represent various minority voices and can help articulate what is working and not working when parents either fail to come forward for a variety of reasons, or if they are not asked. If we are truly interested in whether or not our students are succeeding, we need to engage the various groups our work impacts. I will speak more about this in the district evaluation section below, but having a solid plan that the majority of teachers embrace, becomes a lot more powerful when we include other voices to the goals and the plan.

ELE Program Evaluation

Third-party evaluations are a good idea and healthy for any program or organization. Getting outside opinions from stakeholders such as parents and from impartial parties, colleagues, and experts can be an invaluable experience for your program because they can truly address the issues needing attention, and provide energy and support to improve. Having experienced two extensive outside reviews myself, I have seen the great benefits of going through this process.

Program reviews are however complex and multifaceted. The goal in this section is not to tell you how to conduct one, necessarily, but outline key aspects to consider while putting one together.

Engaging district leadership.

A key aspect of putting together a district program review is to engage district leaders and establish common overarching project goals. What are the reasons for conducting a program review and what are the outcomes you hope to achieve? The Executive Team in your district consisting of the superintendent and her/his cabinet, might play the ultimate decision-making body, but creating a broader leadership committee involving principals and district coordinators, EL staff, and so on, will be helpful in understanding the issues and developing shared commitments and goals. In Salem-Keizer, for example, we had a larger leadership team come together, establish commitments and generate a central question as an initial activity.

The commitments we generated, "We value and support our English Learner Programs – because it is the right thing to do, and because the law requires it," served as our foundation - one that would be referred to at different times throughout the process. In addition to these commitments, we also defined two goals:

1. English learners are our highest priority in our three programs: ESOL, Two-way Immersion, and Transitional Bilingual.
2. We are committed to research-based, high quality language instruction for our English learners

After we discussed and came up with our goals, we then focused on developing a central question to guide the next steps: How can SKPS make the best use of its limited resources (staff, instructional resources, professional development) to ensure equitable access to high quality language education for its English learners? Forming this question allowed our leaders to articulate goals to schools around equitable access within the context of our existing resources.

Engaging in this work as a team also helped create a sense of shared purpose, and it provided a sense of urgency which had been missing in our district dialogue until that point.

Choosing Third-Party Facilitators

A third-party evaluation can be a valuable learning experience for a number of reasons. First, having someone from the outside is important for credibility reasons alone. For example, your leaders might have all the best intentions in the world and want to seriously roll up their sleeves and solve problems; if the perception from teachers and others in the district differs, however, from your intentions based on past history or a perceived lack of transparency, then having someone outside the district leading the discussion will be seen in a positive light. Second, an unbiased person provides a safe zone. People will feel they can speak openly and safely with someone not connected to district leadership, and this is what you need for valuable feelings and thoughts to be shared. A third reason involves expertise. People involved in this work bring specific knowledge and new ideas and insights. They can lead and even challenge leaders to think a different way. I remember showing one of the experts we hired my equity statement with pride only to have her question our wording a little. This led to a really healthy discussion among the team which ultimately led to an improved definition.

Creating a structure for program review

Once you have a third party facilitator hired and a leadership team established with some initial goals, another key aspect to consider would be forming an advisory committee consisting of district licensed and classified staff, community partners, and parents representing different several different language groups. While your district executive team and your broader leadership team might make the ultimate decisions concerning changes and the use of resources, etc., the advisory committee's purpose is to learn about the existing programs and then provide input as to what they would like to see changed or improved.

In Salem-Keizer, our Advisory Committee was comprised of over twenty members of the Salem staff, community organizations, and parents. They provided authentic input from a diverse range of contributors and they served as a steering committee to help form the direction of our programs.

Project timelines

Setting timelines throughout the year with the contractor and the various committees might seem like an obvious step since contracts require them, however, I think it is still good to mention them here. As this process can take the better part of a school calendar year, it is important to think through what meetings and processes need to be organized in advance, so that everyone has it on their calendar and to ensure rooms can be set aside, materials ordered, notices sent, etc.

You will no doubt have your own ideas about the work, but I am providing you with a sample of a partial timeline we used in one of our reviews:

January:

- Review program documentation
- Draft district EL program descriptions
- Establish project goals
- Plan for Advisory Committee Meeting #1
- Facilitate Advisory Committee Meeting #1

February:

- Conduct three School Focus Group Listening Sessions
  - Steps: Engage outside facilitator
    - Arrange interpreters
    - Gather input and translate as needed
    - Input analyzed by contractor
    - Analyze input from Advisory Committee Meeting #1 and listening sessions data
- Plan for Advisory Committee Meeting #2
- Facilitate Advisory Committee Meeting #2
- Analyze input from Advisory Committee Meeting #2

March:

- Formulate draft recommendations
- Plan for Advisory Committee Meeting #3
- Facilitate Advisory Committee Meeting #3

As you can tell by the sample above, a great deal of organization had to be planned in advance. The paid contractor wouldn't necessarily be at every function, but you could discuss where having them included might make sense, and budget accordingly.

Articulating Project outcomes

When working with multiple stakeholders in education, it's really important to be transparent and open to learning and changing. We actually formed a goal around increasing transparency and inclusiveness in district decision-making around EL programming, by creating the following outcomes:

Outcomes: Leadership teams

– Provide stakeholders with clarity of understanding with regard to:
  – Who at the District-level was guiding the program review process
  – Timelines, goals, and desired outcomes of the program review process
  – The expectations, roles, and responsibilities of stakeholders in the process

The above example is just one of several our team created, but we placed so much importance on transparency that we wanted to call it out in our outcomes for all of our stakeholders to see. We really were interested in good honest feedback about our programs so that we could improve, but not everyone invited to the table automatically believed that. That is why we wanted to call it out from the beginning. This may or may not apply to your situation, but you will have other outcomes you may want to spell out prior to bringing together your groups.

Capture recommendations

However you decide to put groups together and collect input, at some point you will have a set of recommendations from which to sort through. The key here is twofold: Again in the name of transparency, you want to communicate the compiled recommendations to your various stakeholders. Secondly, you want to find common themes and prioritize these recommendations into action items that can be accomplished given your current resources. Quite possibly, you may have numerous recommendations and for example, one of those may involve increasing your two-way immersion schools from 5 to 20. While that sounds great, it isn't always a reality to grow in that way given the resource limitations districts often encounter. Still, however, leadership can take common themes and apply them into a set of five to ten action items and then create a plan for implementation as described in the next section.

Create a plan and staying focused

Now that you have input from diverse perspectives and recommendations on how to improve, it really comes time to completing your blueprint. You should have a well articulated vision that will be your focus over the next 3 to 5 years. Multiple stakeholders, including parents, students, teachers, community leaders, and administrators should see themselves in the plan and feel like they are part owners of it. This is a plan that should be able to continue regardless of who leaves the district and who comes on board. It should be articulated in phases and integrated into all of the work the district engages in related to professional development priorities, curriculum & standards alignment and articulation, teacher hiring, attending to the social emotional support of students, title funding support, etc. It all relates and should be interwoven in all district work.

Conclusion

Remember the **core values** stated in chapter 1: To be focused on **equity** in a way that puts the needs of your ELs and other disadvantaged students at the forefront. To be extremely **focused and intentional** in all that you do to ensure that the success of your ELs is a shared responsibility and they are not forgotten or seen as a sub-group that needs support by a small department or a few individuals. To always be **results oriented** and asking the hard questions - is what I'm teaching or is what we are using as a method to serve ELs, working? To be **guided by theory and research** for what is best for ELs acquiring another language and not taking the next attractive program that may or may not be appropriate for an ELD class. To be **grounded in the law** and ensuring all ELs are receiving the opportunities designed for all students. Finally, to ensure that we are attending to the human being, in what I have coined, **Continuity of Care.** These are children who are coming to school hoping to learn and feel accepted. They want to be loved and they want to be given the same opportunities as everyone else. That is, after all, their right as human beings.

ACTIVITY SUMMATION - Putting it All Together

As we come to the end of this book, let's review the activities and consider where we are in the ELE Blueprint creation process.

In chapter 1, you discussed your core values as they relate to serving ELs and other disadvantaged youth. Articulating your values served as your foundation and lead to the creation of a mission statement and several goals.

In chapter 2, you created a set of overarching categories under which all of your ELE Blueprint work will be housed and clearly communicated. You also developed a communication structure that allows for receiving input and making decisions.

In chapter 3, you organized your community advisory group meetings in order to gain input from a diverse body of stakeholders. You perhaps also created a Data Story to show at your first meeting that helps outline the work ahead.

In chapter 4, you had intentional discussions about your professional development structure and how focused it is on the needs of ELs and other disadvantaged youth. To this end, you had your group answer a set of questions to evaluate your current model. You also had leadership discussions with the intent of forming an agreement as to several leadership initiatives that you would adhere to across the district.

In chapter 5, your team looked closely at the ELD classes in your district to see how they are functioning and what supports are needed to make them the most engaging, rigorous, and helpful classes they can be.

Likewise, in chapter 6, you had discussions around how language is supported across content area classrooms. These discussions and the discussions around professional development should be intertwined.

Finally, in this chapter I went into greater depth around the evaluation process and provided some examples from evaluation work I was involved in. As I've mentioned throughout this book, these activities are meant to serve as suggestions and supports. Every district is unique and has different ways of approaching program reviews and planning. My hope, however, is that these activities have helped structure discussions and processes so that you can successfully build a guiding blueprint to serve English Learners. They are, after all, a vital part of our future.

ACTIVITY: Creating a 3-5 year plan

Once you have received input from various stakeholders and have created a draft ELE Blueprint document that reflects your values and goals in several overarching categories, it's time to create a plan that will be implemented in phases over a 3-5 year period. My suggestion is to have the ESOL Director and his/her staff create a plan and submit it to the Leadership Committee, and then to the Cabinet Leadership Team for final approval.

As you draft your plan, please consider the following suggestions:

Create a project management table that shows the blueprint categories and articulates the work to be done in year one. Include goals that are measurable and timely and create a robust evaluation process of that work by March. You will want to see what progress is being made and then adjust the plan for year two.

Create a Strategic Plan and/or visuals that communicate the ELE Blueprint work so that all teachers can share in the vision and be able to articulate it in general terms. Ensure PD opportunities mention the vision of the Blueprint and have your leaders talk about this at monthly staff meetings. To come alive, it needs to be seen and felt throughout the year. Teachers and other stakeholders need to see that the district is serious and committed to serving ELs over time, regardless of who leads. The ELE Blueprint should be viewed as a living, breathing document that is always evolving.

Maintain the existing advisory committee or create another smaller advisory committee that will come together each spring to review the work of the ELE Blueprint and provide input. Having a committee meet each year helps hold the district accountable to the agreed upon work, and maintains a built-in parent and community voice to guide your progress. My suggestion is to have one of the school board members sit on the committee so that she/he can hear what the parents are saying and monitor what progress is being made.

Reference Page

Best Practices for ELLs: That Work in all Classrooms for all Students. Northwest Regional Education Service District. Retrieved from http://ell.nwresd.org/node/42

Brown, H. D. (2014). *Principles of language learning and teaching: A course in second language acquisition.* White Plains, NY: Pearson Education.

California Department of Education. Title III FAQs. Retrieved from http://www.cde.ca.gov/sp/el/t3/title3faq.asp

Crawford, J. (2004). *Educating English learners: Language diversity in the classroom.* Los Angeles, CA: Bilingual Educational Services.

Crawford, J. (2011). Frequently Asked Questions about Reauthorization of the Elementary and Secondary Education Act (ESEA) … and the Policy Issues at Stake. Retrieved from http://www.diversitylearningk12.com/articles/Crawford_ESEA_FAQ.pdf

Cross, T., Bazron, B., Dennis, K., & Isaacs, M., (1989). Towards A Culturally Competent System of Care, Volume I. Washington, DC: Georgetown University Child Development Center, CASSP Technical Assistance Center. Retrieved from http://files.eric.ed.gov/fulltext/ED330171.pdf

Cross, Terry L., and Mareasa R. Isaacs. *Towards a Culturally Competent System of Care.* Washington, DC: CASSP Technical Assistance Center, Georgetown U Child Development Center, 1992. Print.

Collier, V. P., & Thomas, W. P. (2014). *Creating dual language schools for a transformed world: Administrators speak.* Albuquerque. Fuente Press.

Colorin Colorado! A bilingual site for educators and families of English language learners. Retrieved from http://www.colorincolorado.org/

DeNavas-Walt, C. and Proctor, B. (2014 Current Population Reports Issued September 2015) Income and Poverty in the United States: P60-252. Retrieved from https://www.census.gov/content/dam/Census/library/publications/2015/demo/p60-252.pdf

Escamilla, K. (2014). *Biliteracy from the start: Literacy squared in action.* Philadelphia: Caslon Publishing.

English Language Proficiency Standards. Council of Chief State School Officers. Retrieved from http://www.k12.wa.us/migrantbilingual/pubdocs/ELP/WA-ELP-Standards-K12.pdf

Gándara, P. (2015) The Impact of English-Only Instructional Policies on English Learners. Colorin Colorado. Retrieved from http://www.colorin colorado.org/article/impact-english-only-instructional-policies-english-learners#h-lessons-learned

Gandara, P. C., & Hopkins, M. (2010). *Forbidden Language: English Learners and Restrictive Language Policies.* New York: Teachers College Press.

Goldenberg, C. (2013) *Unlocking the Research on English Learners What We Know—and Don't Yet Know—about Effective Instruction.* American Educator, Summer

Goldenberg, C., Coleman, R. (2010). *Promoting Academic Achievement among English Learners: A Guide to the Research.* Thousand Oaks, CA: Corwin Press.

Goldenberg, C. & Wagner, K. (2015) *Bilingual Education: Reviving the American Tradition.* American Educator, Fall

Hart, B., & Risley, T. (Spring 2003) The Early Catastrophe: The 30 Million Word Gap by Age 3. American Federation of Teachers. Retrieved from

file:///P:/BluePrint%20for%20Success/Support%20Docs/Articles/
TheEarlyCatastrophe.pdf

Hattie, J. (2009). *Visible Learning: A Synthesis of Over 800 Meta-Analyses Relating to Achievement.* New York, NY: Routledge.

Jensen, E. (2009). *Teaching with poverty in mind: What being poor does to kids' brains and what schools can do about it.* Alexandria, VA: ASCD.

Klein, Alyson. (2016). No Child Left Behind: An Overview. *Education Week.* Retrieved from http://www.edweek.org/ew/section/multimedia/no-child-left-behind-overview-definition-summary.html

Klein, Alyson. (2016). The Every Student Succeeds Act: An ESSA Overview. *Education Week.* Retrieved from http://www.edweek.org/ew/issues/every-student-succeeds-act/index.html

Krashen, S. D. (1987). *Principles and Practice in Second Language Acquisition.* New York, London, Toronto: Prentice-Hall Intern.

Krogstad, J. & Hugo Lopez, M. (June 25, 2015) Hispanic population reaches record 55 million, but growth has cooled. *FACTTANK: News in the Numbers.* Pew Research Center. Retrieved from http://www.pewresearch.org/fact-tank/2015/06/25/u-s-hispanic-population-growth-surge-cools/

Lau v. Nichols. (2004-16) U.S. Legal.com. Retrieved from http://education.uslegal.com/bilingualism/landmark-legislation/lau-v-nichols/

Linton, C., & Davis, B. (2013). *Equity 101: Culture.* Thousand Oaks, CA: Corwin Press.

Marzano, R., & Waters, T., (2009) *District Leadership That Works: Striking the Right Balance.* Bloomington, IN: Solution Tree Press.

National Association of School Psychologists (n.d.) Retrieved from
http://www.nasponline.org/resources/culturalcompetence/
definingcultcomp.aspx

Nieto, D., (2009) *A Brief History of Bilingual Education in the United States*,
Perspectives on Urban Education. Spring. Retrieved from http://t.urbaned
journal.org/sites/urbanedjournal.org/files/pdf_archive/61-72--Nieto.pdf

National School Reform Faculty. Harmony Education Center. (n.d)
Retrieved from http://www.nsrfharmony.org/free-resources/protocols

OPB (Producer). (2013, February 12). The Importance of the 14th
Amendment Today [Video file]. Retrieved from http://www.pbs.org/video/
2334361038/

Payne, R. K. (2005). A framework for understanding poverty. Highlands,
TX: Aha! Process.

Phelan, C. & Wren, J. (2005-6) Exploring Reliability in Academic
Assessment. UNI. Retrieved from https://www.uni.edu/chfasoa/
reliabilityandvalidity.htm

Saunders, W., Goldenberg, C., & Marcelletti, D., (2013). English Language
Development: Guidelines for Instruction. *American Educator*, Summer.

Staehr, D., Segota, J. (n.d.) Standards That Impact English Language
Learners. *Colorin Colorado*. Retrieved from http://www.colorincolorado.org/
article/standards-impact-english-language-learners

Talk Poverty. (n.d.) Retrieved from https://talkpoverty.org/basics/

The Civil Rights Act of 1964. (n.d.) Constitutional Rights Foundation.
Retrieved from http://www.crf-usa.org/black-history-month/the-civil-rights-
act-of-1964

The Elementary and Secondary Education Act of 1965. (n.d.) The Social Welfare History Project. Retrieved from http://www.socialwelfare history.com/programs/education/elementary-and-secondary-education-act-of-1965/

U.S. Department of Education Office for Civil Rights. (2000) The Provision of an Equal Education Opportunity to Limited-English Proficient Students. Retrieved from http://www2.ed.gov/about/offices/list/ocr/eeolep/index.html

U.S. Department of Education Office for Civil Rights Programs for English Language Learners. (n.d.) ED.gov. Retrieved from https://www2.ed.gov/about/offices/list/ocr/ell/edlite-glossary.html

U.S. Department of Education. National Evaluation of Title III Implementation: Report on State and Local Implementation. (May 2012) Retrieved from https://www2.ed.gov/rschstat/eval/title-iii/state-local-implementation-report.pdf

Wright, Wayne E. (2010) Landmark Court Rulings Regarding English Language Learners. Retrieved from http://www.colorincolorado.org/ell-basics/ell-policy-research/important-ell-court-cases

Wright, W. E. (2010). Foundations for teaching English language learners: Research, theory, policy, and practice. Philadelphia: Caslon Pub.

C1
Salem-Keizer ELLs and the Oregon Diploma Requirements:

Content Area	Oregon Diploma Req.	ELL – Level 3 (Freshman)	ELL Level 4A (Sophomore)	ELL Level 4B (Junior)	ELL Transition (Senior)
Language Arts (Composition)	1		• ELD IVA • 1 Comp. Credit	• ELD IVB • 1 Comp. Credit	
Language Arts (Literature)	3	• Literature III • 1 Lit. Credit	• Literature IVA • 1 Lit. Credit	• Mainstream L.A. • 1 Lit. Credit	• Another Lang. Art or Elective
Math	3	• Algebra I – S • 1 Math Credit	• Geometry • 1 Math Credit	• Algebra II • 1 Math Credit	• Another Math or Elective
Social Studies	3	• 20th Cent. I – S • 1 Soc. Studies Credit	• 20th Cent. II • 1 Soc. Studies Credit	• Gov. / Econ • 1 SS Credit	• Another SS or Elective
Science	3	• Life Science –S • 1 Science Credit	• Physical Sci. – S • 1 Science Credit	• Science Elec. • 1 Sci. Credit	• Another Science or Elective
Wellness	1	• Well. Skills I – S • .5 Wellness Credit		• Well. Skills II • .5 Well. Credit	
PE	1	• PE – 9th • .5 PE Credit	• PE – 10th • .5 PE Credit		
Elective: Fine Arts / Applied Arts / Foreign Language	3	• Elective (Heritage Spanish / Pottery / etc.) • 1 Arts or For. Lang Credit	• Elective (Heritage Spanish / Pottery / etc.) • 1 Arts or For. Lang Credit	• Elective (Heritage Spanish / Pottery / etc.) • 1 Arts or For. Lang Credit	
Other Electives	6	• ELD 3 • 1 Elective Credit	• .5 Elective (opposite of PE)	• .5 Elective (opposite of Wellness II)	
Credits Remaining for OR Diploma	24	17	• 10	3	0 = Diploma Req. Fulfilled

Summer School→ .5 credit classes in ELD / Math / Social Studies / Science →   accelerate path to graduation

Notes:

- **All** teachers (Sheltered and Non-Sheltered) hold appropriate content area licenses/endorsements. IE. Language Arts, Math, Science, etc. (Sheltered Teachers' licenses/endorsements attached)
- At North Salem and McKay High Schools, Salem-Keizer has transitioned level 3 and 4 students **out** of Sheltered classes and into mainstream classes for Math, Science, Social Studies and Wellness Skills. All other high schools will follow this model in the 2012-2013 school year.
- By their Senior year, equal to mainstream English speakers, ELL Transition students' schedules will vary according to their history of success in previous courses. If they pass all classes and graduation requirements (State Writing and Reading Assessments) then they only will need three elective credits and may opt for late arrival / early release / early college classes. If they have failed any classes or need extra assistance to pass Oregon Writing / Reading Assessments, they will be placed in appropriate classes to meet these requirements.

C2-1

C2-2

Salem-Keizer Public Schools
Secondary ESOL Blueprint
2015-16

The Secondary ESOL Blueprint is Salem-Keizer's plan for getting our English Learners at the secondary level, achieving at or above grade level across district schools, and prepared to graduate.

This vision statement is divided into seven overarching categories, under which, all efforts on their behalf is being made.

Our goals are led by the State's Annual Measurable Achievement Objectives (AMAO's), which require every district in the nation show progress in three categories (See below). Our program is assessed and evaluated by ODE based on our improvement towards these goals.

In addition to our AMAO objectives, we have other goals that are less dependent on state test scores. These goals, like equity, 'continuity of care' and bilingualism, for example, are also captured in their respective categories in the blueprint below.

AMAO TARGETS

AMAO 1 – 2014-15 ODE TARGET: 48.5%
Increase the percentage of ELs in the district that are on track to obtaining English proficiency within six (6) years based on a growth model as set by the Oregon Department of Education to 50% by June, 2015.

AMAO 2(a) Goal – 2014-15 ODE TARGET: 9.5%
Goal Met
AMAO 2(b) Goal – 2014-15 ODE TARGET: 27.0%
Goal Met

AMAO 3 Goal 2014-15 ODE TARGET ≥ Level 4
Increase the Math and Reading targets to 50%ile based on ODE Growth Level Cutoffs for ELs in the district by June, 2015.
The district will achieve Level 4 graduation rate based on ODE Growth Level Cutoffs as found on the district Report Card.

1. Supporting Quality Instruction:

Essential Question: To what extent are our ELs receiving instruction in a way that allows them to master content in all core and ELD subject areas?

Essential Question: How do we know that our ELs are increasing their knowledge and ability to understand, speak and write using a higher language register?

Activities: (District ELAS support these activities)

- ELD trainings for new teachers
- ELD support and professional development for veteran ELD teachers
- Strategies that Promote Engagement and Learning (SPEL) trainings for content area teachers
- District PLC: Bring all ELD teachers together to plan and learn together as one team
- AVID EXCEL – Program development for five Title IA Middle Schools
- SPEL Observation Tool – To assist administrators with Legends observations
- Equity – ELAS to infuse concepts and definition in all trainings
- Combining all PD for ELs using common AVID language and work to build several common routines across schools that support ELs with academic language usage
- Jeff Zwiers Training – October 9

2. Curriculum

Essential Question: To what extent are our ELs engaged and challenged in their ELD classes with the instructional materials?

Activities:

- Support our new ELD curriculum adoption through district-wide PLCs
- Observe classrooms using new curriculum to partner in the work and learn how to support

- Continue to support teachers in the development of 'Backwards Design' planning
- Continue to help identify standards for teachers to focus on in their curriculum and instruction.
- Continue to develop our online curriculum Weebly Website

3. Standards

Essential Question: To what extent are teachers incorporating the 10 ELP standards into their daily planning?

Essential Question: To what extent are Curriculum PA's incorporating ELP standards with their CCSS communications?

Activities:

- Continue to partner with curriculum PA's on sharing standards and providing district PD
- Continue to meet and plan with ODE on a shared rollout process.
- Meet with Level Directors and brainstorm ideas for continued rollout

4. Supports and Interventions

Essential Questions:

To what extent are high schools supporting the emotional needs of English Learners?

To what extent do schools feel supported by the ESOL Department at Instructional Services?

To what extent are systems in place to support all ELs?

To what extent are we providing positive messaging to our ELs and supporting their dreams and ambitions?

To what extent are we supporting dual identified students?

- Continuity of Care Initiatives at all high schools – focusing on the issue of long-term ELs
- Data Stories – providing principals with snapshots of data that tell a story about their EL population
- Contributing Voices Conference – Providing positive messaging to all incoming 9th grade ELs.
- SATEL – Providing a voluntary school review to gauge learning climate for ELs in schools
- SPED/ELL – partner with Student Services in identifying students and their language support needs. Identifying ELPA in IEPs and exempting strands where appropriate.
- Newcomer Center Guidance: Revising the guidance for middle school
- Parent Involvement and communication: conduct more parent informational meetings
- Provide focus and support to the Dual Language Program. (See DL Blueprint Outline)

5. Accountability, Evaluation, Assessment

Essential Question: How do we know we are making progress with our goals?

Activities:

- Data Teams: Data team meets monthly and creates 'data stories' for schools to help show progress and need.
- Listening sessions: Continue conducting listening sessions with various groups to evaluate progress.

- Surveys: Create and send out surveys to gauge how supportive the ESOL department is and how it can improve.
- ELPA: continue to exempt students from strands where necessary
- To formulate linguistic goals (bilingualism, biliteracy, English acquisition)
- To evaluate completion (graduation) goals; social (school climate)

6. Leadership

Essential Question: To what extent do our administrators have the knowledge around effective ELD and sheltered practices and can provide coaching to staff?

Essential Question: To what extent do our administrators feel supported in their work relative to EL academic achievement?

Essential Question: To what extent are other key personnel communicated with relative to the ESOL Program and the needs of ELs?

Activities:

- Create presentation on ELs to deliver
- Meet with principals regularly to discuss ELs and blueprint progress/how we can support
- LTEL Workgroup – meet quarterly with HS Asst. Principals, coaches, etc., regarding the improvement of long-term ELs.
- Communicate annually to registrars, counselors, etc., re: ESOL changes and overall vision
- Admin. training on SPEL
- K-12 Articulation efforts

7. Research

- Program Evaluation – Claude Goldenberg – follow up work from his report
- Problem of Practice Memo – Feedback from Problem of Practice Group – continued articulation and planning.
- Continued validation of SATEL Tool
- Continued professional development: AVID EXCEL; Steve Ventura; Anita Archer; Jeff Zwiers. Follow up planning and conversations relative to this work.

C2-3

ESOL BLUEPRINT RUBRIC FOR STAFF			
CATEGORY 1: SUPPORTING QUALITY INSTRUCTION			
ESSENTIAL QUESTIONS: *Essential Question: To what extent are our ELs receiving instruction in a way that allows them to master content in all core and ELD subject areas? Essential Question: How do we know that our ELs are increasing their knowledge and ability to understand, speak and write using a higher language register?*			
Sheltered Instruction Professional Development goals			**ELAS will provide trainings to teachers and build capacity in the following areas:**
Activities	Initial	Beginning	Accomplished
Classroom Strategies for Grouping & Accountability – **all content areas**	Teachers receive initial training on grouping and accountability; they receive 3 instructional routines to incorporate into teaching immediately.	Teachers try new routines but are inconsistent in applying and may need more support. Teachers are not seeking out support from coaches.	Teachers establish new routines to get students talking on a regular basis in groups and they are holding all students accountable. They seek support from coaches. They can produce data to show results of these efforts.
Deepening Academic Conversations in **Mathematics**	Math teachers receive initial training on acad. conversations in math; they receive 3 instructional routines to incorporate into teaching immediately.	Teachers try new routines but are inconsistent in applying and may need more support. Teachers are not seeking out support from coaches.	Teachers establish new routines to get students conversing on a regular basis in groups and they are holding all students accountable. They seek support from coaches. They can produce data to show results of these efforts.
Going Deeper with Academic Conversations Interactive Strategies for **Social Studies**	SS teachers receive initial training on academic conversations; they receive 3 instructional routines to incorporate into teaching immediately.	Teachers try new routines but are inconsistent in applying and may need more support. Teachers are not seeking out support from coaches.	Teachers establish new routines to get students conversing on a regular basis in groups and they are holding all students accountable. They seek support from coaches. They can produce data to show results of these efforts.
Supporting English Language Learners in **English Language Arts**	ELA teachers receive initial training on academic conversations; they receive 3 instructional routines to incorporate into teaching immediately.	Teachers try new routines but are inconsistent in applying and may need more support. Teachers are not seeking out support from coaches.	Teachers establish new routines to get students conversing on a regular basis in groups and they are holding all students accountable. They seek support from coaches. They can produce data to show results of these efforts.
CATEGORY 2: STANDARDS			
ESSENTIAL QUESTIONS: *Essential Question: To what extent are teachers incorporating the 10 ELP standards into their daily planning?*			
Standard Implementation Across Content Areas			**ELAS will provide trainings to teachers and build capacity in the following areas:**
Activities	Initial	Beginning	Accomplished
Building awareness of new ELP21 Standards and getting teachers to use these in their planning	Initial presentation to: MS principals HS principals ELD teachers Program Assistants Instructional Coaches Staff meetings PLC's	ELD teachers meet together with coaches and plan units with ELP21 standards. Content area teachers (math, sci, ELA) begin to meet and plan using ELP21 standards with Common Core State Standards	Teachers are using ELP21 standards alongside CCSS in their unit planning and in their PLCs consistently. Individually, teachers are looking at these standards and the proficiency rubric when planning. Cooperatively teachers are finding time to meet and plan together with ELD teacher/s.

C3.1

Survey Sample Questions

System Survey Sample Questions: ESOL Coordinator and Staff

On a scale of 1 to 10, with 10 indicating Strongly Agree and 1 indicating Strongly Disagree, please respond to the following questions:

1. All students in the ESOL Program receive a dedicated block of time for ELD services regularly. _____
2. The communication between ELD teachers and registrars/counselors across all middle and high schools results in careful strategic placement of students in ELD and core content classrooms. _____
3. EL's are placed by Language Proficiency Level with few exceptions in large program schools. ____
4. Language Proficiency Levels 1 &2 are separated from Levels 3 & 4._____
5. English learners are in mixed-ability classrooms and then grouped by English language proficiency specifically for ELD instruction. They are not segregated from the rest of their English speaking peers._____
6. There are systems in place to ensure that student content and language performances are being monitored. _____
7. Letters are sent to parents each year, informing them about placement in ELD and progress towards exiting._____
8. Level 3 and 4 students and their parents are aware of what they need to graduate and they understand how to get out of ELD._____
9. Students are purposefully and strategically 'clustered' with teachers who have been trained to use sheltered strategies._____
10. An ELD teacher or other staff member is responsible for overseeing placement and monitoring students who have exited the program._____
11. EL students who are also identified as special needs in a self-contained classroom are receiving ELD support in some manner._____

12. Students who are new to the country and are at the very beginning stages of English language production, have a system of support established that will help them quickly acquire language and honor their cultural background and experiences.____

13. All district ELD staff and all administrators understand the exiting criteria and apply it evenly across all schools.___

14. Provisions are in place for alternatively exiting ELs who cannot for some reason pass the state assessment, but who show significant aptitude and success in core classes.____

15. Progress towards graduation for all ELs is being tracked and monitored. ____

16. Staff is having conversations with EL students and parents about their progress early and consistently. ____

17. Every EL student takes the annual language assessment, as required.____

System Survey Sample Questions: Teacher Groups

On a scale of 1 to 10, with 10 indicating Strongly Agree and 1 indicating Strongly Disagree, please respond to the following questions:

Standards and Curriculum

1. I am satisfied with the ELD curriculum overall.
   - The materials are appropriate for the grade level I teach. _____
   - The materials are appropriate for the language proficiency level of my students. _____

2. My students find the instructional materials
   - engaging. _____
   - useful. _____

Supporting Quality Instruction

3. I have the time necessary to plan and prepare for my ELD classes.

_____

4. I have received excellent professional development for teaching ELs.

_____

5. The district supports my professional development._____
6. I feel supported by my principal_____

Supports and Intervention

7. The district does an excellent job focusing on the needs of ELs. _____
8. Our district has excellent systems in place for placement of students.

_____

   ○ All ELs are in both ELD and in core classes _____
   ○ All ELS are with teachers who use sheltered strategies. _____
9. ELs are well supported academically in content-area classrooms.

_____

10. District teachers are
    ○ culturally aware. _____
    ○ sensitive to the needs of students coming from a different culture.

_____

System Survey Sample Questions: Instructional Coaches

On a scale of 1 to 10, with 10 indicating Strongly Agree and 1 indicating Strongly Disagree, please respond to the following questions:

Leadership / Supports & Interventions

1. The district is focused and intentional towards the success of its ELs.

_____

2. As an instructional coach, I feel supported by:
   ○ District leadership. _____

     ○ School leadership. _____
3. Our district has excellent systems in place for placement of students.
     ○ All ELs are in both ELD and in core classes _____
     ○ All ELS are with teachers who use sheltered strategies. _____
4. My position is focused on delivery of professional development for ELs and coaching. _____
5. I feel successful as a coach. _____

Supporting Quality Instruction

6. ELD teachers have adequate time to plan and prepare for their ELD classes. _____
7. ELD teachers across the district are effectively planning for and delivering ELD. _____
8. Teachers across the district are culturally aware and change their instruction to meet the needs of students coming from a different culture. _____
9. Teachers across the district are focused on student learning. _____
10. Core content teachers are using sheltered strategies with great fidelity:
     ○ In middle school. _____
     ○ In high school. _____

System Survey Sample Questions: Parent Groups

On a scale of 1 to 10, with 10 indicating Strongly Agree and 1 indicating Strongly Disagree, please respond to the following questions:

Note: You will want to make a copy of this survey in the language/s of your parent groups.

Key Terms:

English for Speakers of Other Languages (ESOL) Program

English Language Development (ELD) – The class within the program

Instruction & Support - Part 1:

1. I understand why my child is in a class called English Language Development (ELD). _____
2. I understand how my child can exit the ESOL program. _____
3. I understand what my child needs to do to be successful in ELD. _____
4. I understand how I can help my child be successful in ELD. _____
5. My child speaks highly of his/her ELD class. _____
6. My child feels engaged and challenged in his/her ELD class. _____
7. My child feels valued and respected in school. _____
8. My child's language and background are valued. _____
9. My child feels safe at school. _____
10. My child is on-track to graduate from high school. _____
11. My child feels supported and successful in:
    ○ Math _____
    ○ Science _____
    ○ Language Arts _____
    ○ History _____

Support - Part 2:

12. I feel welcomed at my child's school.
    ○ Elementary School. _____
    ○ Middle School. _____
    ○ High school _____
13. Front office staff speaks my language.
    ○ Elementary School. _____
    ○ Middle School. _____
    ○ High School. _____
14. Important information in my language:
    ○ Is posted in the hallways and front office. _____

- ○ Is sent home. _____
- ○ Is well written. _____

15. The school principal is welcoming and I feel comfortable speaking with him/her.
    - ○ Elementary School. _____
    - ○ Middle School. _____
    - ○ High School. _____
16. I feel comfortable voicing my opinions and concerns. _____
17. The district listens to my needs and concerns. _____
18. The school seeks my opinions and involvement. _____
19. Teachers have communicated with me or my spouse about my child in positive ways. _____

System Survey Sample Questions: Community Groups

On a scale of 1 to 10, with 10 indicating Strongly Agree and 1 indicating Strongly Disagree, please respond to the following questions:

1. The district is focused on the success of its ELs. _____
2. The district actively listens to the concerns of parents. _____
3. Schools do a good job of communicating to parents who speak a language other than English. _____
4. The district actively communicates and listens to the concerns from the community. _____
5. The district's schools are friendly, welcoming places. _____
6. English learners receive the support they need to be successful. _____
7. **Short Answer:** In what ways can the school district improve its communication with community stakeholders on behalf of educating its English Learners?

_____

_____

_____

_____

System Survey Sample Questions: Student Groups

On a scale of 1 to 10, with 10 indicating Strongly Agree and 1 indicating Strongly Disagree, please respond to the following questions:

1. I understand how English Language Development (ELD) class is meant to help me. _____
2. I understand how I can exit out of the ELD class. _____
3. I understand how to be successful in ELD. _____
4. I feel engaged and challenged in my ELD class. _____
5. I feel valued and respected in school. _____
6. I feel that my language and background are valued. _____
7. I feel safe at school. _____
8. (high school students) I am on-track to graduate from high school. _____

9. I feel supported and successful in:
   ◦ Math _____
   ◦ Science _____
   ◦ Language Arts _____
   ◦ History _____
10. Generally speaking, my teachers make it fun and easy to understand the material. _____
11. I understand what I am expected to do for homework. _____
12. My classes are easy to understand. _____
13. I know what I am expected to learn in every class every day. _____
14. My teachers like and respect me. _____
15. I have a quiet place to study at home. _____
16. I am on track to graduate. _____
17. Adults in the school are helping me prepare for college. _____
18. My education is preparing me for college. _____

Made in the USA
Columbia, SC
28 January 2019